Chapman 96

George Bruce: Poet 2

ISBN 0 906772 94 X   ISSN 0308-2695   © Chapman 2000

Chapman

4 Broughton Place, Edinburgh EH1 3RX, Scotland
E-mail: editor@chapman-pub.co.uk
Website: www.chapman-pub.co.uk
Tel 0131–557 2207 Fax 0131–556 9565

Editor: Joy Hendry   Assistant Editor: Gerry Stewart
Volunteers: Valerie Brotherton, Belinda Cunnison, Hannah Eckberg,
Dan Hackney and Claire Thomson.

Submissions:

Chapman welcomes submissions of poetry, fiction and articles provided they are accompanied by a stamped addressed envelope or International Reply Coupons

Subscriptions:

	Personal		Institutional	
	1 year	2 years	1 year	2 years
UK	£16	£30	£20	£38
Overseas	£21/$35	£39/$65	£25/$43	£47$75

THE SCOTTISH ARTS COUNCIL

National Lottery Fund

Printed by Inglis Allen, Middlefield Road, Falkirk FK2 9AG

George Bruce: Poet 2000

George Gunn

I often liken George Bruce's presence in the Scottish literary scene to that
of a headland, Kinnaird Head in fact. His poems have that granite feel, tempered with a seemingly effortless lyricism which leaves you in no doubt
as to their origin. The North-east has a long, proud tradition of balladry, of
story-telling and the very essence of poetry itself. Indeed the canon of Scottish poetry would be unthinkable without the strong inclusion of the
'muckle sangs', both of land and sea. So it is into this rich heritage that
George Bruce steps full-blooded, pedigreed and more than able to bring
that tradition on. Now, as he would admit himself, in the autumn of his
years, his gift shows no sign of weakening or wavering. A keen eye and
the clear sense of the worth of a word, for the sake of meaning only, for
the ultimate effect, are what characterises his poetic style. I can think of no
writer who is better at it. Not that Bruce would consider he's 'at' anything.
For example in his poem 'Moss Agate', where the 'thing' is described thus:

> As if the North green-weedy sea
> had entered in and met the South,
> unctuous and vinous, suffusing reds
> with subtle lights of plum.

Described in such a way that the reader can almost taste the 'thing'.
Bruce's work displays many such instances of this certainty, this colour,
but also, as in all art, there is an opposite direction being traced, often in
grey or sometimes, for maximum effect, in black and white. This is from
his poem 'Departure And Departure And . . .'

> Someone is waving a white handkerchief
> from the train as it pulls out with a white
> plume from the station and rumbles its way
> to somewhere that does not matter

What does matter is the journeying and throughout the work there runs
a theme of leaving, of returning, of the impossibility of actually going
back, of what American poet Anne Sexton termed "that terrible rowing".

> The first tomorrow for me began that day,
> the first time my father took me, aged 7 years
> to Bruce's Look-out. It was the first time
> I saw the edge.

That 'edge', of course, being The Broch, Fraserburgh, where the rolling
farmlands of Buchan pour themselves into the North Sea which itself
stretches further than the eye can follow. Here these piscean tensions are
acted out both in memory and in language, where everything must be
accurate and shorn of sentimentality, where the effect, the 'thing', the
sought-after clarity, can sweep like a lighthouse beacon across the page
and the imagination. So the beginning of the poet's journey is described:
"Home: bed: nor-east corner: night winds beat/ about the granite house".

One is reminded of Stevenson's Leerie, forever lighting the imaginative
lamps of boyhood. It is Bruce's use of Scots in 'On The Edge', in particular,

Portrait of George Bruce (1) by Colin Dunbar

which washes his poetry clean, like the sea across the Fraserburgh sands, but at the same time the language conveys that sensuality of his early Broch years, when it was normal to marvel and when everything was an adventure and where everyone had a definite origin.

> "Ye're a grander", glowered the fisher loon
> at me and I glowered back. I niver thocht
> ither than the Broch loon I wis like ither loons.
> "The rocket's up." Bang, bang it gaed and his
> at squeel and a body doon the streets gan gyte
> tae mak the herbour. Force 9 gale and a boat
> in trouble, and afore we're there the lifeboat's awa.

If this shares a certain resonance with passages from the Neil Gunn of *Morning Tide* and *The Silver Darlings* then it is only because both writers share a common background of communities who know only too well that a living which is drawn from the sea can as easily forfeit a life back to the hungry sea. Comparisons can also be drawn from Christopher Rush's collection of short stories about life in the East Neuk, *When Peace Comes Dropping Slow*, when the young Venus Peter shouts at the sea, "Yer greedy!". In his use of Scots Bruce seems more assured, more willing to let his imagination and memory take flight, more ready to inhabit dreams and sensations. The English, on the other hand, is much more grounded.

> Our granite house
> by the sea – never
> out of its roaring or
> shushing or hacking cough –
> stood steady as a rock.

The world, for George Bruce, is a certain place where the air is for breathing and life is a broad canvas where the writer must notice accurately for himself first and foremost and then for 'The Lave', that beautiful Doric word which is almost untranslatable, but means roughly, 'everybody else'. As he puts it in his long poem study of Cezanne, 'Pursuit' "Accept he must/ To reject is to reject all". As was said of Cezanne, "When he painted a mountain he painted an apple. When he painted an apple he painted a mountain". With Bruce, on the other hand, you know that when he is writing about an apple it is definitely an apple he is writing about.

This thingness of 'things' could become, in lesser hands, a tyranny. The pulse of his work represents a liberation of 'things', an affirmation of life, of poetry, of art. His poem 'Cliff Face Erosion' which is a response to the rock photography of Orlando Gaultieri, memorably puts it:

> I am old, yet the breathing intimacies
> of air, those inspirations from the forever
> fresh wildernesses of the sea, even the sea pink
> I picked from the marram grass as child,
> has carried through the years unfearful,
> trusting, secured through time into this now,
> this moment of putting pen to paper as if
> this wholeness, indestructible, outdated
> time and gave us a permanence of being.

Even in this tension, creative certainty, but none-the-less Calvinist, if not

Portrait of George Bruce (2) by Colin Dunbar
Printed with kind permission from the National Portrait Gallery

existential, there is always doubt. In 'Epistle to Edwin Morgan', Bruce asks:

> BUT doubt steps in between
> the pen and the paper as to whether
> any good could come from a body
> too young for my age.

And he answers himself in another epistle, this time to John Bellany, where he concedes "That's the wey it is".

This placing in time and space, as if the writer were obsessed by the world and cannot do enough to celebrate it, but always with discipline, goes some way to explain his fascination with painters. Cezanne, Willie Gillies, John Bellany, all furnish the poet's mind with searching, investigating meditations, as if he recognises the superiority of painting, an art form which can claim the silence, "Creating that final word aspired". But in the poet's ear there is the north-east voice which warns "So watch your step this mornin/ my mannie". The 'thing' is the level-headed world of harbour walls and ploughed fields, much as Bruce quotes Rilke on Cezanne, that he had "the incarnation of the world as a thing carrying conviction". George Bruce's work may indeed inhabit that Rilkean 'House of Being', but the house is made of granite, square on to the sea.

His first book *Sea Talk* was published in 1944. Fifty years later we have *Pursuit*, from which the poems quoted are taken, by the way of *Landscapes and Figures* (1967), *The Red Sky* (1985), and *Perspectives* (1987). He is still writing. If Scotland's passage through the 20th century has to be charted then we could do no better than to use the poems of George Bruce as a guide, for as he wrote of Velazquez,

> He turned the searchlight of his mind
> upon each and every object equally,
> persons or thing as if each in its
> difference, might through the precision
> of line and paint, each weighed in the
> balace of mind, would yield final truth.

To understand that there is no final truth is the poet's tragedy. To articulate the space between the two silences which bracket life each writer attempts differently. As he writes again of Velazquez "he heard the silent talk of the star, and it became humanity", so can be said of Bruce.

It may be too grand a claim that poets construct 'humanity' but we should at least ask them to add to its greater stock. The life, work and sheer energy of Bruce is a result of a dedication to the art of poetry few can sustain or hope to match. His greatest achievement, I think, is in attaining that serenity which comes when an individual comes to terms, as best they can, with their own mortality. In a haiku at the very end of *Pursuit* the poet says

> The sea trembles – voiceless,
> It is a rare moment
> when a word is sought.

Rare indeed. For George Bruce, quite natural. Younger poets can only learn and if Bruce affirms Yeats in that regard it is a lesson well learned. Scotland, recently, has lost too many of her finest poets. Let us celebrate George Bruce, his life and work, as he lives and works on.

George Bruce

How to Hang a Big Picture
for Sue and Mike Adler

First make up your mind to get married
to the right person, otherwise no matter
what you do it will remain askew.
Then engage a Professor of the History
of Art, who will apply herself to right angles,
while a Master of the History of Fine Art
applies himself to left angles. Add in
the artist, one bald antiquity, plus
one bustling child, as spectators,
critics, applauders, loungers on sofas,
and all is set for the containment of form,
and this form is alive with creation –
snake-shapes, box-shapes, dice-shapes,
running lines, jumping dots, spaces
interrupted by weighty components
that float in a sky, high, – all held
together, awaiting the great uplift.
DONE. Hold breath. It stays on wall.
When the house is asleep each
pulsing piece slips from its picture
place and dances silent on the floor.
Morning. Two stare at the painting.
It is ringed with happiness.

Translation of above: *I shall be happy to attend the Warriston celebration of your wedding on Saturday, 16th October 1999.*

Immigrant

A met him aneath the Hielanman's Umbrella.
It wis dingin doun: said he bided Maryhill.
He'd been aboot a bit – his faither
yince Rabbi at Minsk. (Mair likely Tomsk,
a thocht:) traivelt tae Germany, got
the bairn oot quick. Atween then an Glasgow,
lang time. That's his tale, bit oot's moo
cam Glasgow – aa Glasgow. It wis Setterday.
Noo, fit wid a Russian Jew support, Celtic
or Rangers? "The Jags," he said. O coorse,
a thocht – Partick, that's far he comes frae.

A Birthday Gift from John Bellany
A Painting of Eyemouth near the mouth of the river.

John
You took my breath away
and gave it back ten times over.
What day-light here!
What dance of light!
caught in a mind that still
could believe meaning, life-giving
meaning, could still be here,
here in your magnanimity,
in the truth of your imagination,
and you send me this great gift.
At least it's given to one who
fifty-eight years ago wrote these
words about another place,
Did once the sea engulf all here and then
at second thought withdraw to leave
a sea-washed town?
Sturdy the houses, biggins sea-resistant,
boats hammered sea-worthy –
all bathed in light.
House and boat, sweep of road-way,
bright, alive with sea-borne airs.
It is an air that blew away
each particle of dust,
each human blemish.
It goes about and about and I
am in it, rejoicing in this quick
of life of colour and always the eye
taken up and blown sea-wards.
I leaped in my childhood.
My age has gone: I leap again.

George, 26/2/2000

Hamish as Interrogator
sketch of a generous mind as revealed in
Elegies for the Dead in Cyrenaica

"There were our own, there were the others.
Therefore, minding the great words of Glencoe's
son that we should not disfigure ourselves
with villany or hatred . . ."

'All Bathed in Light', a birthday gift from John Bellany to George Bruce, Eyemouth Harbour, Berwickshire – March 2000

A captured German officer is before him.
Captain Henderson puts the required
questions concerning military matters.
Interview ended, but hardly begun.
He is speirin aboot's bairn-time,
aboot sangs sung lang syne
in anither place. Noo he is nae sodjer-man
tae the tither, nor tither tae him. An the
officer-chiel is harkenin to nae sough
o daith i the desert, an at the hinner end o't
the officer-chiel says, as Hamish pit it doon:
Africa changes everything. In reality
we are allies, and the desert our common enemy.
Bit there was aye a coorse wun blawin.
As Hamish put it: *in this landscape of half-wit/*
stunted ill-will. It brewed no ill-will in him
and in the Seventh Elegy he made
a sma lament for Seven Dead Germans:
> *Seven poor bastards*
> *dead in African deadland*
> *(tawny tousled hair under the issue blanket)*
> *wie einst Lili*
> *dead in African deadland*
>
> *einst Lili Marlene*

And the song was for everyone.
And when Hamish saw the birds
go north from Africa they were
carrying their songs for Scotland,
and when he went north through
Italy he was at one with partisans
and freedom-fighters and he became them
and always there was the searching mind
through the complexity of ideology
and the contradictions of history
but never ending in that dry desert.
These were the crucible out of which
through passionate reflection came
poems and songs which went
to the healing of broken Scotland.
So we salute the makar, adventurer
and singer – Hamish.

These lines were spoken by George Bruce at a party organised by *Chapman* and
Shoots and Roots, Edinburgh Folk Festival, on 20 November, 1999, to celebrate
Hamish Henderson's 80th birthday.

Returning to the Broch

In Memoriam Robert Bruce

The place of your birth and growing-up
is never the same on return.
In the beginning God made it for ever.
The South Church stands bright
in the morning sun. Even the Central School
in its grey granite sparkles. Remember
the cold rock pools at low tide, providers
of partans, greenbacks, cumpers, flukes
destined for the blue pail in the hand.
I would pour them back in the water
in that time, and again I am in that time
now and no storm raves in my forever . . .
Now there is another present by me and he
would have them back in their places
one at a time, for he would know
what happened to each, and why?
They told me – he is your brother.
He is the one who would know for sure,
Yet all to me was wonder and strange,
and he, child, barely into his teens
said, "There is no God. I am an atheist."
And no-one paid much attention and I,
devout in ice-cream, am running
and jumping, and leap so long, so high,
I am ten minutes in air before
I found touch down. "Rubbish," said my brother
and ran fast through the years but
deliberately, stopped, briefly, as he met
Hegel (Plato was always with him). When
in the middle years of 'the dismal science'
– and our people broken – Marx thrust
his solution upon him. Robert sent
Das Kapital to our father, who read it,
expounded it to the makers of barrels
as they thundered the iron hoops about
wooden staves as small fires of shavings
glowed, encircled by barrels to hold herring.
They, coopers, were not enamoured
of his presentation. "This," he said, "was
matter for debate." And so it was and
always at the dinner-table – mid-day dinner.
I return. I see great skies, terrible seas.
Upon the retina of the brain, printed,

a boy, naked, is swept in white water
raging round a rocky point. He would
hold to the stone, but the back-wash
has him. Gone, till the forward power
of water again and again sweeps up
the body. "Run!" bawled Robert. "I'll run
for help." I stay and watch a drowning.
This I store from time long past.
We return to the table to debate.
By the way he had met Confucius.
A point of beginning, but you
cannot be with Confucius without
being at one with his talk. So
he is there, and with Buddha,
far from the appetites of the West,
where nothing is allowed just to be
itself. Where place and the hand that put
on the writing surface – Taoism, Buddhism,
Zen, Basho travelling with his pack of Haikus,
he was there and in the tongues of
Canton, Mandarin, Hokkien, Hakka,
to be applied as suited, and he
half-blind, but seeing a continuum,
discovering an essence, like the bee
to the flower, not one kind of flower,
to make the sweetness of honey.
So he would return, perhaps not
knowing why, to that rugged source –
the Broch, to that place, which,
as child he made his first rejection
in four words: "I am an atheist."
Now half-blind, then blind, he
returned with two words: the Christ.

This day 2nd October 1999
I stand in Kirkton Kirkyard, amongst
the bones of my ancestors and think
of the brave spirit of Robert.

Robert Bruce (1911-1999), diplomat and Oriental scholar, at one stage in a varied career mainly in the service of the British Government, was Principal of the Government Officers' Language School in Kualalumpur. He taught Cantonese and Mandarin, on which he wrote two books, and edited books on Hokkien and Hakka. Later he learned Thai for his post as representative of the British Council in Bangkok. For his post of Cultural Attaché to the British Embassy in Hungary he became fluent in Hungarian.

L' Annunciazione

Beato Angelico, San Marco.

The illusion could hardly be
more distant from the facts.
In some rough hut or cave
or byre the usual pain and he
emerges bloody, squalling
into this world. What if
the truth was in the illusion,
and out of our time the universe
that casually threw this planet,
presents the contradiction.

Today, Tomorrow

When I saw you on my door-step
I was in danger of being happy
while cruelty and misery possessed
this globe. To the blind politicians
killing was an acceptable mode
of life in circumstances of necessity,
dressed up, of course, in special words:
"We act to save the nation: a just war:
Our bombs precision bombs, selective:
the tyrant's forces broken, in disarray.
We finished him off. The burned homes
will be replaced, and all will be as was."
Look at Dubrovnik, the old town by
the Adriatic sea, at peace with itself.
Moslem and Catholics sat at cafe tables
in the street; converse in slow walk
in the street: for this the street was made.
It was enough to be mere human kind,
neighbours were neighbourly; visitors
were at home. War came. They made
a nothing of the street. Ended,
they put it together again as it was.
Picturesque as it was to the eye.
The people were back in place, and sat,
and walked, but in each head death sat
and walked, and when each saw each other
saw each as if forever other, no longer kin.
They walk the street erect: they talk correct:
The guard is in their tongue: the guard

is in the eye, in case they see and know
that they are kin. O let the children dance
their wayward dance. Around and around
they go, and the dead street floods with
laughter as they pour from thresholds of home.

The Breaking of Barriers

Our tomorrow grows from the bud of today,
would flourish in all who would walk
new ways, not saying 'no' to yesterday
when the seed was planted, yet not bound
to that past, but open to fresh new airs
that blow down barriers, unite our being
in common humanity. We see anew our selves
in others, others in our selves. Quick,
quick, open your heart and mind to all kind.

*These lines were written at the request of Malcolm MacKay as a summary of
an idea for* Law At Work. *They may also apply to the breaking of the barrier of
the Berlin Wall 10 years ago.*

The Picture
Homage to Hisashi Momose who makes permanent the moment

Sometimes one sees a painting
In an Exhibition. You cannot pass it
and move to the next and next
for you are held in its stillness.
Lift your eyes from it and move
down the stairs and a new beauty
is in their simplicity. You have heard
the earth has exploded, but that
is in another place. Step outside
and the square is right for what
it is meant to be, its formality
is what good squares must have.
Even the blue of the sky is tempered.
There must be a deal of virtue around,
but who played that card? Was it
the painter, or the conjunction of the
right companion preparing the way
to look at the product of a delicate hand.

The New Scottish Poetry Library
Dedicated to Malcolm Fraser, Architect

First there was its silence. Each true
building has its silence, particular to
itself and purpose. There is a command
to the entrant. "Wait," and allow stone
and wood and light to utter soundlessly.
By-passing the outer ear this keeper
of written thoughts, gave two words
to the hearer – 'limpid clarity'. Once
years and years ago I looked through
the transparence of sea water
of the rock pool to the white micacious
sand of its floor, across which a small
crab moved its articulated limbs to
the cover of a strand of wrack at
the pool's edge. The gleam of a
small stationary fish despite its sculptured
stillness insisted life was here, and in the tremble
of tide the pink anemone swayed. The wonder
of a world of light – fact and vision one thing –
unasked, presented itself, but here now
the directive to build a new poetry library
was explicit. Here to be contained
was a repository of personal and national
experience in the medium of that
rhythmical concentration of words,
known as poetry: but the conventional concept
of the isolated scholar in semi-dark drawing
light into himself, is not the dominant note here.
The whole stone building is a response to poetry –
a visual poem in itself. The wild light upon crags and sea
bursts in a blaze through rounds of ceiling apertures.
There leaps to mind a voice singing:
"Were na my hert licht I would dee."
This capsule of light has taken into itself
laughter and the deep grief of Cresseid:
"Fader, my mirth is gone." Light has no weight:
it may be hard, strong, gentle, fierce, kind –
all here, it runs with the flow of stairways:
it pin-points a table top bright with books
for bairns, Shafts of light beam their way
to book-shelves. A hand reaches and
the inner world's nutrition becomes hers.

She has taken to herself *Deer on the High Hills*.
This light has the limpid clarity of enlightenment.

The Fox and Lucina

Happenings in back-gardens by the Water of Leith

*So long they looked it was as if eternity
had entered in our mortal world.*

One fine Spring morning I looked
upon my patch of rough green grass,
arid he was there, sunilit. Rarely
had I seen a creature with such poise,
in sleep, for so the animal, brown coat,
with white under-belly, appeared to be,
until I noticed one ear at the ready,
pricked for threat of danger, survival.
I could not move for any movement
of mine was cumbersome against his
most delicate engagement with earth.
Then, undisturbed, the visitor was
on the wall. Gone, and I was
the poorer for his absence. He
looked in from time to time, but I
was no priority – and then, no more.
He had gone elsewhere, as I discovered
as I told, with some small boast, Lucina,
(who is as fair as is her name) "My fox,"
she said. More orderly than mine, he preferred
her green place with the stream running by.
No posture of sleep for him. He
looked around, alert, took in all.
One day she went to the open door.
He rose to his feet. He did not go away.
He looked at her and she at him for long.
There was no fear nor hating
in his eyes, and no enmity in her,
for she knew his beauty honoured
the earth they shared.

More of Colin Dunbar's artistic work can be seen on page 88

Holiday Money

Linda Cracknell

When he squatted next to me on the beach, the first thing I noticed was his arm. The curve of biceps began just above the elbow and led inside the sleeve of his 'Hard Rock Café T-shirt.

"Hi Lady. You like cigars?"

"No thanks. I don't smoke."

"Maybe your husband?" He searched the immediate area with his eyes.

"No husband." Dead.

"You take some for a gift, for a friend. Special from Cuba."

"I don't think so."

"Very good price. In the shops $80. I give you for $25." Ah, handling stolen goods then. Forget it, my boy. He brought out of his shoulder bag a wooden box decorated with two figures touching fingers over a balcony. He placed the box just above my knees as my legs stretched out on the sun-lounger. I was suddenly conscious of my middle-aged flesh rolled out like uncooked pastry in front of this boy in his, what – early twenties?

"See. Romeo and Juliet."

"Very nice." But no.

He leant towards me, unfastened the clasp at the front of the box and raised the lid, releasing an aroma of something like horse-shit. Rows of cigars like brown sausages were tucked into neat lines inside. He pulled one out and put it into my hand. It felt dry and flaky. Hours of Cuban sun had been rolled into it. He had a good marketing technique. They did here. From where I was sitting, I could hear the sales pitch of the cocktail barman, singing, *"daiquiri, piña colada, Cuba libre"*, from under his thatch on the beach. He coupled the rhythm of Tito Puente with the grit of a London newspaper seller.

"Very nice." I closed the lid and handed the box back to him. We smiled at each other. I hoped he had accepted my refusal but he wasn't moving on to the next sun-spread tourist. I noticed he had slumped back from the squat into the sand so that he was now sitting next to me, his shoulder bag between his feet. We both looked towards the sea.

In front of us a man had beached himself, his belly doming high towards the sun. It was shiny with sun oil. The pharmaceutical coconut smell was cloying even from here. His arms were spread wide, his head low and unsupported on the sand. The extremities of his arms and legs flapped slightly. I hoped he wasn't stuck. I didn't feel like effecting a rescue.

"German?"

"No. English."

"Ah. English. Is a good country, no? You like Cuba?"

"Love it."

"You like to see some famous places?" He turned his gaze inland. A pile-carpet of forest was rolled out over sharp mountains. The buildings of the town aspired up to them. "Churches, sugar mills. Very old. I take you. I know very well."

"I don't think so. Thank you."

"In town, there's very nice restaurant my friend runs. In his house. Very good food. You like fish?"

"Yes. But I get all my meals here." I waved my hand behind my head at the ship-like hotel grounded on the beach behind me.

"Lady." He reached forward and fingered the immovable plastic wristband clamped on me by the hotel when I arrived. "This doesn't mean you can't leave here. You're no slave to this place."

His thumb and finger dented my wrist. And as our hands were side by side, there lay the contrast between the colour of his skin and mine. My eyes skipped up to his. How could I help being flattered by his attention? And then Carol seemed to appear at my elbow, in her sensible shoes and business suit saying, "Mother, what exactly do you think you're doing?"

The heat and humidity squeezed me even more in the town. I took a break from exploring the patios, plazas, and towers and headed for the smoked glass air-con cool of the dollar shop. I grabbed a bottle of *agua mineral* and joined the queue of dollar-rich Cubans which trailed along the glass case towards the till. The cool brought back my brain a little. I cast my eye over what the fortunate could buy. Rose-scented soap, lipstick, matches, cigarette lighters, jelly, biscuits, and towards the back of the shop, microwaves, fridges and electric fans with big price tags. A man left the shop and walked away down the street with a toilet bowl on his shoulder competing in height with his straw hat.

The queue shuffled forwards as each conversation at the till came to a natural close. As I waited, delighted to be slow in the cool, the sound of hooves on cobbles took my attention through the glass shop front onto the street. I still hadn't got used to the novelty of the neat ponies who carried men in broad-rimmed hats and spurs through the streets. The view of the pony was obscured by half a dozen people clustered around the door, faces contorted in the effort to view the shelves. One of them, nose and forehead squashed to the glass, hands splayed above his head to blacken his reflection, looked familiar. He was wearing a 'Hard Rock Café' T-shirt. It was the boy from the beach.

As I came out onto the pavement, the heavy dampness of the air, the smells of food cooking and rotting fruit wrapped themselves around me, strait-jacketed me. I had only been in the air-con a few minutes but had already become unaccustomed to the street.

"Hey, lady! Remember me?" His long limbs bounded towards me along the pavement. He was taller than I'd realised before, his face shaded by a baseball cap.

"Yes. From the beach." We shook hands. It was almost like meeting a friend in the street at home. And it was good to have a reason to stand still for a moment.

"You buy water only?" He put his hands to his shaking head. "Lady, you could buy, anything . . . the world!"

I looked back into the shop. Rose-scented soap was not the pinnacle of my dreams.

"Yes, but I can go shopping at home."

"Of course. Is easy for you." He looked back through the shop window for a moment. "You can buy bluejeans in your country?" He slapped his thighs as he said 'bluejeans'. His smile radiated enthusiasm. I felt myself reflecting it back at him.

"Yes."

"Ah. Levi's – they the best, no?"

"So my children tell me." And he nodded, a look of longing on his face as he pondered the slimfit status they would give him.

"Let's go. I show you the town." And it was a change to have a companion to walk with. But Carol came along too. Stalking along just behind us. Frowning.

Later that afternoon I wrote postcards by the swimming pool, sitting well back from the edge to avoid the tidal waves as twenty or so German women surged and wobbled through an aquarobics session. "Today I had a guide to the town," I wrote, "A young man". Bound to get a reaction with Karen and Louise. The dreadful duo. They flashed in front of me, arms folded, smiling and nodding 'I told you so' at me. "See what a bit of Cuban rum and holiday spirit can do for your love life, girl." It was all very well for them, they were a good bit younger than me. But the fantasy invaded my body. It took root and grew as the afternoon heat thumbed my eyelids down. It was not unwelcome.

It's night. But there's some soft light, from a candle perhaps. And the room opens onto a veranda or a balcony through which wafts the palm tree rustle, the croak of harmless insects and jasmine scent. My shoulders are bare and have a soft (young) sheen in this light. And his T-shirt fabric clings and slips over the slope of his chest. We're relaxed. Drinking something. Opposite each other at a table. My body acts for me without preparation. I put my hand on his and continue to talk, as with one of my fingers I trace the long muscle from wrist to elbow, turn at the elbow and continue under the edge of the T-shirt sleeve over the taut skin on his upper arm. The skin is black satin, woven oil. I span the strength of revolutionaries with my hand. And somewhere in between then and the bit where we're in bed, the clothes come off. Invisibly. With the noise of silk static. And his voice in my ear is mango, sliced with a silver knife. There's cloves and coffee on his breath. When I kiss the dip in his chest, there's sea-salt and spray. The night is like chocolate liqueur dripped drop by drop onto my tongue.

And as my eyes refocused on the glare of white-backed postcards slipping sweaty across my lap, there was a thunderous rumble of rocks as my mother turned in her grave.

"You have to go to the *valle de los ingenios*. Is very interesting. Very old.

Many tourists like." He was in the hotel lobby, waiting for me two days later.

"What's 'ingenios'?"

"The place where they made sugar. The rich people. Let's go. I take you." Not long afterwards, I was in the back of some fifties American car driven by a friend of his. The windows in the front were open and he rested his elbow high on the door top and flashed smiles back at me. I sat low in the back. Despite the rips in the leather seats out of which grey stuffing escaped, I felt the breeze catch my hair, remembered some ancient sensation. Could it be of glamour? Probably not. Carol would say that was ridiculous. I was in a dangerous situation.

The rear end of the car seemed to sink and trail as we graunched out of town. We swerved to avoid the cyclists, horses and carts and the people waiting. What was it they were waiting for? The road rose and fell in a straight cut between sugar plantations. The dense forests of leaves swayed high above the sun-blackened skin of workers in straw hats bent over their machetes. The verges were littered with stringy bits of flattened brown cane. After a few miles, we turned left over a railway line and into the courtyard of a mansion house. Through the windscreen the base of a tower was visible. I climbed out of the car, and the heat which I thought we'd left back in town pressed down on me. As I stood up, my head reflexed backwards to take in the unexpected height of the tower. Like a ridiculous travesty of a wedding cake, it rose, tier upon tier, into the hot white cloud. I felt slightly sick.

"What is it? Or *was* it?"

"For the rich master. He use to watch his slaves."

"Slaves?"

"*Si amiga.*" He picked up my hand and started to pull me towards it. "Come. We climb."

The custodian at the bottom looked at us both and then spoke to me in English. I paid a dollar for each of us then we started to clatter up the wooden staircases. They swayed. I wondered if there was such a thing as health and safety regulations.

"Is it much further?" I asked when Antonio waited for me after three staircases.

"*Poca mas*. A few more." And he sprung upwards on flip-flop feet.

At last we stood in the arched window of the summit, leaning on a sturdy metal grille. I wanted to sit down. Sweat trickled down the inside of both my legs underneath my shorts. Way below I saw the car. Antonio's friend was now sitting on it, leaning back on straight arms, his legs splayed around the silver swan which crested the bonnet. He was surrounded by a small group of girls in micro length shorts. Something white worked in their hands as they chatted. Even at that distance you could see that they had the poise of all young women here. Heads high, backs arched to push the shoulders back and the boobs out. It had taken me a while to realise that the ones in skin-tight lycra grafting themselves to the arms of fat foreign men were prostitutes. Even the ordinary girls had this belief in their bodies. But Antonio was with me. Not them.

A train whistled to our left and we could see it, dinky-style, almost making a bracelet as it curved between the sugar plantation and the cluster of white houses separated by lines of washing and shaded by the spread of mango trees.

"You like?"

"I like the view very much, Antonio." I felt a surge of gratitude. Of well-being. A man wanting to please me. "Thank you for bringing me." I was close to him, in that opposite kind of way. The fantasy trespassed into my waking mind. It would have been the simplest thing to make a bridge between us, to slide off my scarf, the red one, bright with flowers, and capture his neck in it. A simple step to pull his head down to mine. But we slipped sideways out of the possibility. Slipped without even scuffing each other's edges. He started back down the stairs.

As we came back out into the courtyard, the girls who had been around the car clustered around us. Now I could see that the white things in their hands were crocheted goods – tablecloths, shawls, serviettes. They had a towel rack covered in them. A girl with the body of an athlete, her black hair whisked up in a baseball cap and wearing bright white trainers pushed to the front and spoke to me, gesturing at the cloths. She arranged one of the shawls around my shoulders, leaning over me with good-humoured murmurs to pat it in place.

"She ask you if you like to buy some textiles," said Antonio, and stood back, away from the huddle. Just as the heat had pursued me, I felt oppressed by the girls and their cloths, the way they flicked their smiles between me and Antonio and waved the cloths near to my face. There was a sickly smell of something – coconut perhaps. Why didn't Antonio tell them to leave me alone? I pulled at the heavy shawl on my shoulders and pushed it at the girl in the baseball cap, knocking my way through the towel rack and out of the huddle towards the car.

"Hey *amiga*. What's wrong?" I heard Antonio call after me. "You don't want any? Very special to this place."

When I looked back from the safety of the back seat of the car, he was shaking dust off the cloths and returning them to the rack. The baseball girl was flashing her hands and upper body at him but he shrugged and backed off towards the car.

I was hanging my head when he climbed in next to me on the back seat. Tears of frustration, heat and shame were ready to burst out of me.

"I'm sorry. I didn't mean anything," I said, my head still bowed.

"That one." He nodded his head towards the baseball girl. "She my sister. Is hard for us. Our father is ill. We have to try to make money."

I looked up at him. Of course. That was why we were here. Nothing to do with any attraction. Not even friendship. The stupid old woman in me thudded back down to earth. I waved goodbye to my fantasy. It was a bit sad, really. That tugging at the edges of my subconscious had become quite familiar; like a friend.

I had to stifle a laugh when he passed a handkerchief to me. Mopping someone else's tears was a gesture I well recognised as a mother. But this was a mere boy, younger even than my own children.

I didn't use it for a while. I stared down at it, flat and folded in my hands. It was white. Very white. Folded neatly. Pressed, maybe. Was that the sort of whiteness you get from bleaching in the sun here or was it some poor girl with her knuckles rubbed red in a sink of cold water? His mother even? Oh God, maybe his wife. I opened the handkerchief and mopped my cheeks. Antonio looked at me with his head on one side. I thought to give him the handkerchief back but then I saw as I dangled it from my hand that it had a smudge of my lipstick on it. And I don't suppose he would want my tears.

It felt more like a dance hall than a provincial bus station. We passed between the groups of travellers, towards the obvious huddle of western-ers waiting for the tourist bus back to Havana. Salsa music goaded passion out of the crowd. Feet shuffled and pelvises rocked to the beat as people got on with the sociable business of waiting in the holding area before being squeezed onto the buses through a narrow gate. Crowd sweat warmed my nostrils. How was it that it wasn't an unpleasant smell here? It just smelt like an affirmation of living. As I squeezed through, I caught my handbag strap on the neck of a guitar projecting from an old man's back, and nearly pulled it to the floor. It triggered a chorus of laughter from him and his friends. He pulled the fat stub of a cigar from his mouth and waved it at me as he cackled.

Antonio and I found a small area of shade and leant against the rough concrete wall. Before I went through the gate, he kissed me. Once on each cheek. And I thought I caught a faint whiff of raw onion. I was look-ing forward to settling on the bus, starting to relocate the right person in the right body. By the time I got to Gatwick I knew the transformation would be complete and Carol would never guess.

It was cool on the bus. I felt my skin begin to dry, to feel more like it did at home. I might even need a cardigan. He stood next to my window. The brightness of the pink T-shirt I bought him in the hotel shop was muted by the smoked glass. I mouthed as silently as I could, "I'll write," and mimicked scribbling with my hand, "I won't forget the jeans." After all they'd only cost about £35 from Tescos. So my children tell me. And he smiled. The bus started to pull away. He waved and smiled. Smiled and waved. As I put on my cardigan, I found his handkerchief was still in the pocket. No longer pressed and pristine. It was too late to give it back now. I let it dangle. And it felt like the right gesture. I waved the hanky at him through the window.

Once we were out of sight of the station and Antonio, I turned away from the window. Across the aisle from me was a woman of Carol's age. Her legs had been sun and sandblasted to mahogany on the beach. She was looking at me. She turned away as she saw me register it. I thought I saw disgust on her face. I smiled and looked back out of my own window.

Janet Paisley

Come On

Outside, rain
pummles the road,
punishes the last flowers
last flowering.

Birds have more sense
than be out.

Besides it's dark.

The moon left an hour ago.
Winter is washing down
the last leaf of summer.

Earth's blood, the rain.

You've had my anger.
What now, love?

Come on,
let's do it.

Knife

Give me a knife like the wind,
a wind howling high loneliness,
the wind that whistles close and fast,
an ice-blast to scythe cheek to bone.

Give me a knife sharp as song,
pure as the clear note of cut glass,
clean as words that slice the heart,
a knife that drives as deep as that.

Give me the casual knife, a shaft
black-handle snug in the palm,
a knife that peels off thinnest skin,
the knife that pares down everything.

Give me the surgeon's blade,
that sliver of a branding fire,
a slight-slip razor thin and sharp,
the deadly living mirror that is art.

artist

the line is

a lengthening of shadows

when a sun falls away

lit by the flame in you

the line is

mountains to swim through

oceans beating on a skin

a forest fall drumming into

earth seeding her own echo

the line is

drawn between us

while a sky breaks

an eggshell dawn into morning

dreams wakening to touch

all we can make of

the line is

all we can become is

all we can be is

all we are

in a sky ripe for harvest

earth burning in song

of seas to be danced on

the line is

love, is

life, is you

drawing me in

Illustration by Suzanne Gyseman

Sarah: Stranger danger

Ma da says ee's gittin a new caur.
N'ah says see r'at man roon n'corner
s'got a funny motor,
s'got lectric windaes,
s'got a compewur in it,
s'got a wee man in it says
Few-elle is low.
N'ma da says whit've ah telt you?
N'ah says at's no sweerin.
N'ma da says mind yer cheek.
Gaun in strange motors?
Whaur's yer heid?
Whit've ah said aboot gaun wi strangers?
N'ah says s'man roon n'air.
N'ma da says aye, n'at's whit you say!
Whit dae you ken?
Jist you walk hame.
A wee man in it!
Be waantin ye tae go
an see ees puppies next.
N'ah says hus ee got puppies?
N'ma da says Naw, an they never huv.
Onywey, it micht be a rabbit.
but you wullnae see it.
So dinnae you be gaun
in ony mair strange caurs
r'ah'll gie ye the back ae ma haun.
N'en, whin ah came oot the school
is motor stops, ini man says
m'oan you, ah'll gie ye a run hame.
N'ah says naw, ye wullnae.
N'ee says, ae ye stupit?
Git in, ah've no got aw day.
N'ah says spect ye've got a puppy.
N'ee says Sarah, ah'm yer daddy.
N'ah says aye, n'at's whit you say.
Ee skelpt ma lug!
N'ee says at's fur yer cheek.
Noo ye kin walk hame.
Spec ee hud a rabbit up ees jook.

Sculpting

The knife knows what it deals with:
earth, wood or stone. It allows
what it feels to guide the stroke,

always freeing. Blood would run
on this blade were it flesh carved
but this is wood, a knotted root.

The form shakes loose of constraint:
spilled soil, flaked bark, rotted stick
and in the centre what holds good;

man and woman entwined, shaped
underground, by dark, by growth.
I do not pretend to know

what forces make the forests,
nor why stones wait for finding.
Hands see what heart will not admit:

his back is strong, her limbs lithe,
inextricably they writhe
the brutal agonies of love.

Blade

the blade is a solitary pursuit,
a single shaft of light,
the shining edge.

the blade is healer, holier than
water, blood or bone,
it alters what it touches,

cuts without wearing,
grows young sharpened on stone.

the blade is harp, a song
sung by keening wind,
a tune whistled in storm.

its stroke is cleaner than death,
returning its deliverance.

the blade keeps its promises,
does not fear deep, yet
will skim a thin skin off.

teasing, it featherstrokes
a lover's breath on throat

28

whispers its secret,
moonshine light with knowing
self, stark as the shadowless.

you would trade anything
for the shine of it

in your darkness, for the sweep
of freeing kiss, the perfect arc.
treat well with it,

the blade will open up
all tomorrow when you meet.

Brave New World
for the poet Tom Bryan

A fur trapper stalks in his throat,
earthy syllables easy as
the shifting season, patient
as winter for the green spring.

He walks a continent, knows
the perfect arc of fish, life
pooled in brown waters.

A hunter, he moves faster
when still, seeking out
the restless, the sudden shift.

Deeper than wheat in soil,
his eyes speak of mountains
shouldering the sky, tell
when the she-bear comes

acres open wider than a wound,
plains become infertile desert,
endless nowhere to run.

In one hot breath, she comes,
harder than stone, sharper than song,
a forest flood-tide brushing out
air and day, cutting light.

Her drum thunders a blood-beat pulse.
The rush of eye searches shift,
a move that will have him fixed.

Set now for sudden dance,
the man, he dares to stand.
Hunter to hunted, becoming prey
only if courage runs away.

Sandy

Katrina Crosbie

Christ it's cold, wind screaming off the Forth and your fingers numb and still not time for Sandy.

You shouldn't think about him. Getting soft on a punter really fucks you up, Jen says, but you're not soft on him, course you're not, you wouldn't be that daft. Anyway, you've got other things on your mind. There's a car pulling up in front of you, a guy leaning out the passenger door.

How much, petal? he says.

Thirty, you say, thrusting your pelvis forward so that the orange street-light glistens on your black nylon thighs.

He nods and you get in. He drives to the waste ground at the end of Quayside Street, parks and gets in the back beside you. Doesn't say a word, just shoves you down on the seat, yanks up your skirt and gets on with it.

The seat-cover smells of fag-ash and vomit. A quiver of nausea runs through you. *No . . . think of something else . . .* Amy. Amy scented with Pears soap and baby powder, tucked up on Gran's bed-settee, and Gran – your mum – delighted at you getting that job at the casino so she can have her granddaughter all to herself six nights a week.

You start wondering what it would be like if you really did work in a casino and you're off, off to a place with champagne and crystal glasses and you behind the roulette wheel in a lurex dress and Sandy in a dicky-bow, laughing into your eyes, only his laughter turns coarse and guttural, he's grunting like a pig and he's –

Not Sandy. And you're not in a casino, you're sprawled on a stinking back seat with a stranger pulling himself out of you and trying to avoid your eyes as he wipes himself off.

Then you're out on the pavement stuffing the cash down your boots and you're desperate for a drink but you know that wouldn't be a good idea right now. Anyway, it's Sandy next. And you've time for a coffee at the drop-in first.

The drop-in used to be two rooms and a bathroom in one of the Shore tenements before the Council cut their grant. Now it's a minibus. Still, there's a Calor-gas fire, a coffee urn, sandwiches and stuff. It's quiet at the moment, nobody around except Jen at the table in the corner, handing a packet of condoms to a girl who looks about fifteen. If we can't put you off the idea, she's saying, at least make sure you use these. Then she starts banging on about AIDS testing.

You help yourself to a coffee. It's scalding, but you gulp it anyway. With a bit of luck you'll be gone before Jen gets the chance to collar you. She's always going on at you these days. Ever since you let slip about Sandy.

But as you drain your cup you hear Hi, Debs, how're things? And there she is in front of you, all crow's feet and shaggy perm.

Fine, you say. Then: Better get back to business.

Hang on, she says, laying a hand on your arm. I want to talk to you.

Oh? You say.

Ten-thirty, she says. Saturday. Time for Sandy?

Look, you say. It doesn't mean anything.

No? She looks you up and down. It doesn't mean anything when you buy an expensive leather suit that you only wear on Saturday nights? And the new boots? They don't mean anything either? Come on, Debs. I wasn't born yesterday.

It's business, you say. Honest. He's a regular. I'm just keeping him sweet. And you really do believe it while you're saying it. Fantasies about casinos, lurex dresses – ways of getting yourself through it, that's all.

Watch it, she says. That's all I'm saying. Her grip on your arm intensifies. Getting stuck on a punter'll fuck you up, she says. Fuck you up so you won't be able to do it anymore. Not with him, not with anyone. Put you out of this game forever. Unless – she looks at you, chin tilted, daring you to give the right answer – unless that's what you want?

You think about the hundred and fifty quid you could make tonight and the seventy a week the Social was offering then you shake your head.

But Jen, you say as you head for the door. Thanks.

Outside, you see Sandy's white Megane parked in the shadow of the bonded warehouse. Then you're clacking over the cobbles fast as your heels'll let you, opening the door and sliding in beside him.

How are you, Debs? he says, and the mixture of shyness and eagerness in his voice gives you a rush in the pit of your stomach like the one you get from vodka, only better.

Great, you say.

Cold tonight, he says. Making conversation, like civilised people do.

Lovely and warm in here, you say, brushing the back of your hand against his. He leans over and kisses you. But after a moment he breaks off and says Sorry – didn't mean to rush you –.

Shhh, you say, drawing him to you.

For all that he must be in his forties, he kisses like a schoolboy and you can tell he's never made love to a woman apart from yourself. He's told you about how his mother died, how he lives alone in Inverleith, one of those big sandstone houses overlooking the Botanics. What it would mean to Amy to live in a house like that, you think. Go to a decent school.

You move into the back seat, start to undress each other. Then he says wait a minute, love, and reaches for a travel rug and spreads it underneath you. Your heart contracts. It's the consideration. As though you're his girl-friend or something. Someone he wouldn't mind being seen out with one day. And love, he called you. Love.

He's moving on top of you, slowly at first then quickening, murmuring Debs, oh Debs, oh Debs. You move with him, wrap your legs around him, kiss his forehead, lips, throat, hold him tighter and tighter and when your bodies start jerking out of control mouth the words Sandy . . . I love you . . .

Afterwards, he gives you your money. Then he says I've got something for you, Debs. In the boot.

You follow him out of the car. He opens the boot, lifts something out and hands it to you. A rustle of tissue paper then you're standing there cradling a gleaming gold casket with cellophane where the top should be. Inside, there's perfume – Chanel No. 5 – soap, talcum powder, a frosted glass pot filled with something pink, creamy – *Pour le Corps,* it says on it.

Suddenly, you're floundering. Out of your element. Sex – sex is fine. Sex is what you do. But this – I – you shouldnt've. I can't take this. It must've cost a bomb.

His face crumples. Don't you like it?

Course I do, it's just . . . Then you can't go on, because if you did you'd have to say it: *Just not for the likes of me, Sandy.*

What? he says. Not good enough for you, am I? Because the only way I can get myself a woman is to come down here?

No – not that, Sandy –.

He fixes his eyes on a crumpled Carlsberg can in the gutter. I suppose I've always been a dead loss, he says. With women, I mean. But I thought this was different. He walks round to the driver's door, opens it then looks at you. Anyway, he says, a bit too brightly. No reason this should affect our business arrangement, is there? See you next Saturday?

Without waiting for an answer, he's gone.

You feel as though somebody's kicked you in the stomach. You and your bloody fantasies. House in Inverleith – who were you kidding. You're a common prostitute. And Sandy – what does that make him?

You'd like to try and work it out, you really would, but you know that's not an option. It's half eleven; still a couple of hours to go before you can knock off. And you'd better unload that gift box before somebody nicks it.

So you head back up to the drop-in and there's Jen, having a sit-down with a coffee and her knitting.

All right, Debs? she says.

Fine, you say. Only . . . can you look after this till I finish?

No problem, she says, taking the box. Then she sees what's in it and her eyebrows lift. Sandy? she says.

Mm-hm.

She scans your face. You been crying? she says.

Don't be daft. It's that wind. Bloody fierce tonight.

Sure that's all?

Sure, you say. Then: See you later. You give her a wave and a smile.

But as you hit the street your smile disintegrates. Jen was right. It'll be harder now. You'll go on, you'll do what you do because you have to, because the gas bill's overdue and Amy's outgrown her shoes again.

But it'll be hard, you think. Then you force yourself to put that out of your mind because there's an estate car with an open window drawing up beside you. How much? the punter asks.

Thirty, you say.

He nods, and you get into the car.

William Oliphant

A Scottish Soldier's Two-Fingered Salute to Rupert Brooke

If ah should shoot the craw, think only this,
When youse are minus me, that there'll be
Some coarner o' an English pub that hiz
Ma airseprint on its favourite settee,
And there ah'll dwell, on that upholstered pad,
Wi' mony a spirit pint o' bitter taken,
And dreams o' yashmaks shed in auld Baghdad,
And mony a harem-sworn vow forsaken.

Jist think, this hert, all duty shed awa',
On guard at the eternal Sergeant's Mess,
The duty every Scottish hert abhors,
The sichts o' daurk bare scuddies in the raw,
The reel and feel o' Hielan' kiltedness,
An' anither o' they bliddy English wars.

The Villa Nelle

Do not go visiting the Villa Nelle!
Though it stands snug and modest in the glen,
The Villa Nelle is on the road to Hell.

Well-meaning matrons from the district tell
Sensation-seeking strangers: Gentlemen
Do not go visiting the Villa Nelle.

And clerics, under Sunday morning's bell,
Have tipped the wink to church-going aldermen,
The Villa Nelle is on the road to Hell.

While wives, afraid their husbands catch the smell
Of sin, lay down the law, and say again,
Do not go visiting the Villa Nelle.

And some precocious youngsters, growing well,
Are darkly warned before they get the yen,
The Villa Nelle is on the road to hell.

Regard the lissom witches cast their spell,
And cast your soul beyond all human ken,
Do not go visiting the Villa Nelle.
The Villa Nelle is on the road to Hell.

Noah Sonnet

Brocht up, lan' loaked in Asia Minor, ah'd
Nae problem learnin hoo ti spoon ma brose
Avoidin voyages. Though life wis bad,
An bad it wis, afore the watters rose,
Aspite the scunnert, squamish, naushous boak
Engenert bi the very thocht a waves,
Ah quite looked furrit ti the proamist soak.
An built the boat, an press-ganged weans, an slaves
An beasts, an tholed the voamit an the shairn
Slapt in ma face when flung agen the wind,
An gret the seek desperr lik ony bairn
Wha's devil-trodden, tempest-lashed, sea-pinned.

An noo, beached oan this bliddy, drookit Ben,
An hifti start the trauchle ower agen.

My Finest Poem, Maybe

My finest poem may be a villanelle.
Though sonnets often have been all the rage,
The villanelle has lasted rather well.

When Dylan Thomas tried so hard to tell
His dying father to engage in rage,
His finest poem was a villanelle

And William Empson, though disposed to yell
In verses written, page succeeding page,
His villanelles have lasted rather well.

While Shakespeare's sonneteering chimes quite well
Against his blank verses, ranted on the stage;
His finest verse was never villanelle;

And even bawdy limericks, close to Hell,
Admit, between the sexual wars they wage,
The villanelle has lasted rather well.

So when my Muses rise and cast their spell,
And shall my self-doubt finally assuage,
My finest poem may be the villanelle.
The villanelle has lasted rather well.

"... Only the Other Versions of Myself"
Images of the Other in the Poetry of John Burnside

Dag T Andersson

The title "... only the other versions of myself", is taken from the opening poem, 'Halloween', of *The Myth of the Twin*. At a poetry reading John Burnside said almost all his poems could have been called 'Halloween'. What he does in his poetry is an attempt to awaken, to recover or even resurrect the dimly-seen forms and figures which are at the same time strange and familiar, as they arise out of the gaps of loss, of oblivion, gaps we try to fill with some hope. The presence of these pre-verbal figures is a reminder of something we should have seen but could not, something which we lost even before it could awaken the slightest premonition in us. Looking at a photograph of his dead grandfather the poet discovers

> There is something in his face
> of death accepted:
> a recognised form, like the shadow that comes to the door
> and is only the cat,
> the ghost of something
> complex and remote.

Or we face the gap as an echo from a presence that could have been, as a gap which could have given room for a soul, a fellow companion whom we only recognize after having lost him or her as

> ... the sudden, impersonal quiet
> after a death,
> the current slowed, the sense of giddiness,
> the gap between one moment and the next
> where nothing is that could have been a soul.

"For any event there are two images", Burnside says, "the one I choose and the one I cannot avoid". He presents us with an imaginative duplicity rooted in myth. One of his central preoccupations is the origin of our existence in a meeting of the ordinary and of myth. We come upon myth at the edge of ordinary things, and poetry aims at making these forms accessible to us. In our everyday life they are subdued. Ordinary life requires their submission. By radicalising the things and events of ordinary life Burnside makes the forms of myth visible to us. One of the basic myths in his poetic world is that of the twin. His poetry is dominated by what we could call 'twin images'. The twin is always with us, in some guise present, as a version of ourselves, as something we have lost or forgotten. It fills a space in or around us, a space we think we occupy until we suddenly experience that it is haunted by the ghost of another. In Burnside's poetry the self is a haunted spot.

The presence of the other is often marked by our dim ties to the animal world. We are walking in the first winter snow and suddenly discover that what directs us is "a trail of pawprints", leading us to "some animal brightness" in which we see ourselves reflected. Or we receive "the knowledge of an old reality" when we hear "the casual mention in a song of fox".

How we respond to the often pre-verbal figurations of our 'others', our 'twins', is described in the last passage of 'Halloween':

> The village is over there, in a pool of bells
> and beyond that nothing,
> or only the other versions of myself,
> familiar and strange, and swaddled in their time
> as I am, standing out beneath the moon
> or stooping to a clutch of twigs and straw
> to breathe a little life into the fire.

"*Only* the other versions of myself". The little word "only" in this context has no soothing effect. This "only" is not only 'only'. It is rather an indication of serious matters being at stake.

We may trace a motive from the depth and darkness of Romanticist philosophy and poetry in Burnside's encounters with what he also calls "the secret versions of ourselves". In his study of *Hermeneutics Ancient and Modern*, Gerald Bruns claims Romanticism is one of the richest and most critical moments in the long history of struggling with the question of what is happening when we think something or someone is *making sense*. What is it that hits us when we experience something – or someone – making sense to us? Also, what is going on when something or someone stops making sense or is plainly inaccessible to sense – the way most of us are?

Bruns refers to Wordsworth's statement of the task of the poet in the preface to *Lyrical Ballads;* ". . . it will be the wish of the Poet to bring his feelings near to those of the persons whose feelings he describes, nay, for short spaces of time, perhaps, to let himself slip into an entire delusion, and even confound and identify his own feelings with theirs." Wordsworth is fully aware of the drama unfolding in our encounters with the other. His poetical program includes, again according to Gerald Bruns, "a critique of the subject by dramatising its vulnerability to otherness, the abysmal risks that hover and loom both inside and out." We cannot just listen to the voice of others or pick up the text of another as we please, meet the other with the attitude of what Bruns calls "hermeneutical consumerism". If we are to listen or to read seriously we cannot avoid serious transformation. Wordsworth therefore sees the necessity of keeping "distance from others, to preserve self-possession against the demonic character of another's discourse". For: "discourse *is* demonic, possessive, dispossessing".

The thought which Kant and German Idealism opens up, namely that, in our relationship to the world, things and persons are transformed into versions of ourselves is a thought frightening enough. But it is even scarier to face the implications that what we think of as ourselves is only what we can discover in something or someone other than ourselves. It seems very appropriate that the epigraph to his most recent collection, *A Normal Skin* (1997), is Wallace Stevens' words: "When the mind is like a hall in which thought is like a voice speaking, the voice is always that of someone else". As Gerald Bruns points out, Stevens himself tried to overcome this frightening experience of hearing voices by imaginatively reducing heterogenous voices to a single voice.

This voice verges towards anonymity. The main question involved in such an effort, according to Bruns, is whether achieving this aim amounts to getting rid of the human. Perhaps, he asks, losing the human is the price imagination has to pay in order to create works of art? The work of art itself seems to lead us to a kind of otherness where the human is left behind and "seems to cut all ties to human beings" as Heidegger says. Or are we brought to something beyond the human which is necessary to shed light on the question of what humanness is? A main concern of Burnside's poetry is to understand the meaning of Dante's term 'transhumanar'. Do we have to *leave* the human, imaginatively, in order to *raise* the human?

As Romanticism opens up the darker sides of our encounters with the other, Burnside radicalises the question of the sense of the other by stepping into minds at the edge of or even beyond humanness, as he does in his thus far 'darkest' collection, *Swimming in the Flood* (1995), a venture which is carried even further in the investigations of his first novel, *The Dumb House* (1997). *Swimming in the Flood* confronts us with poems where rapists and killers are allowed to speak, and after having been left with a strong feeling of distaste, we discover that Burnside has made us see far enough to be aware of the logic – and even in its distorted way – the rationality of evil. Entering into these 'evil' minds we discover that their acts have something scarily irrefutable about them. We discover that they cannot be excluded from what lies within the boundaries of the humanly possible. Even these minds become 'other versions of ourselves'. By risking to see this far through the minds of others Burnside is opening up for something without which we cannot meaningfully speak of the human. He urges us to ask whether true humanness can be won without risking to lose it. What is at risk in the killer and rapist poems of *Swimming in the Flood* is our concept of the autonomy of the self. At the edge of everyday life, where Burnside's poems often are set, our concept of an autonomous self is constantly being threatened. This concept of identity and self-possession is one of the necessary fictions of everyday life, governed as life is by the rational part of the human soul. Without this fiction we could not go on. Our everyday life does, however, make us short-sighted. As the Danish theologian and philosopher K E Loegstrup has pointed out, the rationality of our enterprising life imprisons our understanding, it curtails it, pares it down. In order to be incorporated into action, our understanding must be shrivelled. This is why what we call 'real life' has a fundamentally *abstract* character. We deal with each other on the basis of an abstraction from the history and the world of the other. This fact, Loegstrup says, can also explain why we treat each other so mercilessly.

In order to gain any kind of autonomy in a meaningful sense of the word, we have to give up the fiction of self-possession and surrender to what Burnside calls the 'neutrality' of the soul. As 'neutrals' we are non-

38

personal, non-local, non-social beings, occasionally even beings with a
'dark' side. What Wallace Stevens attempted to achieve through harmo-
nizing different voices into one, Burnside seeks through what he calls a
"surrender to all life, to the continuum of energy, to all the possibilities of
integration". The killers and rapists of *Swimming in the Flood* are hope-
lessly lost because they have failed to surrender. Instead they resist. They
are persistently self-possessive. As travesties of the rational self they realise what we all risk when we conceal what Burnside calls "the black light"
from sight: we allow it to interrupt again in extreme form. What the distorted form of self-possession and autonomy, the extremity of the rapists
and killers most obviously excludes, is the feeling of strangeness. This
feeling of strangeness is supported first of all by Burnside's use of the
word 'almost', perhaps the key word to his poetry. In 'Winter Holidays'
we are carried through by 'almosts' to a state of neutrality.

> What we will see, looking back
> on this not-quite life?
> How it almost snows
> over Christmas, those webs of white
> dawning across the hills
> and melted by noon,
>
> and how we are almost happy with the lit
> glitter of the tree,
> the stillness that clings to the window
> like moss, and the smell of our own
> warm comfort filling the house
> on long afternoons
>
> till we turn to the nearly blue
> of night on the glass,
> or stand out in the garden looking up
> at circles of counted stars
> and feel ourselves a little strange again,
> neutrals in the mystery of presence.

Although quiet and reticent, there is an alarming tone in his voice when
Burnside speaks of the enigmatic and mystical aspects of ordinary things
– or the ordinariness of the great mysteries. In his poems things are surrounded by a silent space which protects them against the public noise
and allows them to speak with deeper resonance than everyday life normally accepts. We are thus reminded of how we share space with things.
In the poem 'Home Farm' in *The Myth of the Twin* the poet speaks of the
"silence about the house" as "a wider self". His poems recollect what he
calls "the forms we might have known before the names". The silent space
of things is the equivalent to the names". Our taking part in community
presupposes the recognition of our non-personal, non-social "neutrality",
the "otherness" of our self-possessive autonomy. And in a world where
the value of things is at the mercy of our changing standards and calcu-
lations, things need to be rescued from the grip of naming. "There is", Walter Benjamin says, "in the relation of human languages to that of things,
something that can be approximately described as 'over-naming': over-

naming as the deepest linguistic reason for all melancholy and (from the point of view of the thing) of all deliberate muteness." Still it is the linguistic being of man to name things, he continues. The necessity of naming is thus filled with regret and this regret is one of the deepest motives of poetry. Burnside writes:

> I dream of the silence
> the day before Adam came
> to name the animals,
>
> the gold skins newly dropped
> from God's bright fingers, still
> implicit with the light.
>
> A day like this, perhaps:
> a winter whiteness
> haunting the creation,
>
> as we are sometimes
> haunted by the space
> we fill, or by the forms
>
> we might have known
> before the names,
> beyond the gloss of things

Poetry's task is to recover, to resurrect the forms we might have known.

In his 'Occasional Poem for Charity Graepel, aged two months', Burnside reminds us of a state when the mind is nothing more than "a sequence of echoes". When we later learn to name things we have to ignore these echoes. Overshadowed by words we lose sight of things.

> . . . and what she knows of dogs, or light,
> or water, is a mystery to us,
> who have them named and lost, a truth resolved
> in the grammar that clothes and undermines our
> thought,
> and shadows her wonder at this, the impossible world.

Naming is losing. Our speech is only about what we do not have, Novalis says. In his interpretation of Walter Benjamin's essay on 'The Task of the Translator' ('Die Aufgabe des Übersetzers') Paul de Man points out the second, and often overseen, meaning of the German word "Auf-gabe": *task* is also a *giving up*, a surrender. Serious language work requires the task of naming as part of gaining humanness. At the same time it requires a surrender to the loss that is involved in all naming.

John Burnside's images of ourselves as others, his twin images, reveal the task of poetry – and the task of being human – as something that is always accompanied by a giving up, by a surrender to the necessity of losing. In recognising the others as versions of ourselves, we lose ourselves. Thus only can our humanness be gained. His poetry teaches us how to carry with us the dual images of the twin, in order to see. His poetical awareness recognises a strangeness, an otherness of things which by virtue of escaping our choices is able to deepen our view of the world.

John Burnside

In Tromsö

As it should be, the water is black;
black to its very limits, so it seems
the anglers on the quay are reaching in
for something older than the silent fish
they land from time to time: the heft and mass
of shadows they have sensed
and cannot name.
It's something else they want: a cry, a song;
you see it in their faces when they feel
the tug on the line, and a darkness begins to form
at the root of the mind
like one of those mermaid tales
their ancestors told
in the chastening light of summer.
What blackness we know is ours,
but nothing quite explains the murmured song
that comes through the purl of water
– tide-turn or siren voices – nothing explains
the pull of it, or how, once and for all,
we answer.
They listen for this in Melsvik
and Middagsfjellet:
through wind and the year's first snow, a sound like waves,
an animal longing that shudders against a door
in Kautokeino, plaintive as the song
that rouses the chosen soul from work or sleep
in fairy tales.
They hear it through the trees, and put away
their tools: or, in a kitchen, someone stops
to listen, birdlike, perched against the rim
of distance, reaching far into the dark
and finding their other lives, unmarried, lost,
alone in the snow and singing a favoured hymn,
or reaching for a world, while someone else
calls from another room to say, "it's nothing"
– and nothing dispels that echo in the flesh:
it never leaves, it knits against bone,
waiting to be remembered, like salt
of first love, or the scent of goldenrod.

Some More Thought on the Notion of a Soul
(for Corine)

Never the plural. A high barn filled with straw
and the flicker of errant birds amongst the rafters,
a quiet fish-house, open to the sun,
where the packers sit, turned from their work
to smoke, or talk,
a litter of gut and ice on the wet stone floor
or any schoolyard where the children wheel
and turn from their games, as if
catching a sound in the distance
and waiting to hear it swell, to make it out,
a noise like water, say, or gathered birds,
far in the almost-heard, the almost-known
is where it happens, singular and large
and unremarkable, like light, or fire.

Blues

I

It's moments like this
          when the barman goes through the back
and leaves me alone

     a radio whispering
               somewhere amongst the glasses
– *I'm through with love* –

     the way the traffic slows
               to nothing
how all of a sudden
               at three in the afternoon

     the evening's already begun
               a nascent
dimming.

               By ten I'll be walking away
on Union Street
               or crossing Commercial Road
in a gust of rain

     and everyone who passes
               will be you
or almost you
               before it's someone else.

II

or how I feel tonight
    abandoned
        stilled
aware of every nerve
    of every

pin-point of fatigue
    and nursed assent
encrypted angels
    dangling in the blood
acid singularities
    of fire.

The way I am emptied
    for every
and no good reason
becalmed and absurdly
    expert in the art
of boiling a kettle
    or raising a cup
to my mouth

like the night I'd been travelling
    for hours
on a slow-moving train:
snow on the open fields
    the whiteness
glimmering
    mile after mile
        like a child's

impression of infinity
    – the odd
wavering bend in the road
    and a single
mint-coloured lamp for gas
    or a roadside bar.

I was halfway to sleep
or perhaps I had slept
    unawares
then started awake
when the train pulled
    into the station
and didn't move on

and though I was waiting to ask
      no one came to explain
and I sat there for hours
with my face
      to the ice-cold glass

the windows half-reflection
      half-
some vaguely good-humoured
      notion of dissolve

the place-names on the signpost
      almost gone
some local or native word
      for 'hopelessly lost'

III

or how I keep thinking of nowhere
      and meaning you
– spaces you might inhabit
      as the light

inhabits doors
      or windows
          or the bright
membrane of yolk and milk
on the kitchen table –

the way a sound
      – this music
          or the owls'
nightlong to and fro
      of lulls and cries –

rests in the mind for years
      like a childhood dream
whatever remains unfinished:
      the not-pursued
each glimmer on the cusp
      of touch
          or loss.

Continuing City

Paul Brownsey

The image I need is given me as the plane tilts down towards Glasgow. The vast carpet of lights by night is a jewelled Jerusalem, a wonder. But each light in that vast carpet is solitary and tiny. If it went out, the eye would not notice any difference in the great glittering sweep. And so the lives that go on down there are tiny, solitary things, too, entirely dispensable, each of them a pin-prick of light that doesn't really count for anything.

I am about to try whether this image is the truth.

I have met Robert only once, and that was half a lifetime ago, in 1977. *Met.* Is that the right word for a one-night stand?

"Oh, a one-night stand. The perfect shorthand representation of the lack of meaningful human connection in big cities." That is the received opinion. I used to have another angle. I used to say, "Promiscuity is a way of taming the frightening hordes you pass in the streets. You don't know any of them, they've all got lives that are unknown to you, and God! they might be *better* lives than yours! Sleeping with them is a way of cutting them down to size, of making sure that no-one else is happier than you. Only another 863,471 Glaswegians to go – and I'm leaving the women till last."

I remember – what? Straight, very fine blondish hair that flopped about: he will go bald early. A comfortable looseness of flesh that was not quite fat. A cock that wouldn't unshrivel. A mouth that often bore a secret joyous smile accompanied by downcast eyes. Arms that held me and hugged me, again and again. Lots of smacking, puckered-lip kisses. His attempt, as he riffled through my records, to pronounce 'Schütz', and, when I corrected him, his sweet look that said: that's another important thing mastered. Oh yes, and there was a core to him that was separate from everything I could see or hear or touch, like an invisible altar.

I did not suggest meeting again, and though I probably said (for I usually said it), "See you around," I didn't. There were moments when I thought of him; for instance, at a club where the dancers looked over their partners' shoulders to see what other possibilities might be about.

Then at Christmas came a card signed just 'Robert', no surname, no address. I knew it was from him because although at that point I had worked my way through 94 Glaswegians, none of the others had been called Robert; at least, going by what they told me.

There were three crosses for kisses. One would have meant nothing, but three meant a gush of puppylike love. Endearing. He'd addressed it to Mark Down; right forename, wrong surname. Well, there'd been no call to tell him my surname. Down was the name of the flat's previous occupant, an old lady who'd died. When I brought Robert back I guess I hadn't yet got around to removing her brass plate from the door. He's sharp, is Robert.

A year later came a card with "Thanks for everything" in large, painstaking handwriting. He'd wanted to put a personal message but was too clumsy to come up with one that had any application to me. Touching. And now he'd added a surname to his signature, and the address of a flat in Govan: he'd come out to his parents so could risk a card from me. I signed it just 'Mark'.

Two months later it brought me a Valentine card. The front showed a man riffling through stacks of gramophone records. The words ran, "I remember all my old favourites, but best of all . . ." When you opened it, the words continued, ". . . I remember you". This allusion to the Frank Ifield hit from his childhood revealed something constant in him that had not been overthrown by the passing fashions of punk and disco music.

He had written, 'Love, Robert'. He could now send a Valentine card to another man without a hint of jokiness or camp. Another sign of integrity.

I did not respond to Robert's Valentine. I was seeing Stewart, and things were getting serious. Still, Robert's card had its effect. It emboldened me to start living with Stewart, for if things went wrong with Stewart – well, Robert was like money in the bank you've only just discovered is there. As for me and Stewart, that is an entirely different story, one that takes place wholly above the ground in the daylight. It is a story of complete love, unqualified happiness. I am stunned with wonder when I think of it.

Robert's card the next Christmas was meant to put my nose out of joint for ignoring the Valentine. There were no kisses, no love, no address for a return card, just two names intimately linked by an amper-sand: 'Robert & Nigel'. *So there!* The style of the card had changed, too. It was no longer the big tacky glitter-covered card that had been Robert's natural choice. This one had an Old Master Nativity on the cover. Robert had been taken in hand, was being given some of the class he'd always wanted. I could see how a well-spoken Englishman, a bit older, with his own elegant flat, could be attractive to a boy from Govan.

Robert stopped sending cards. This was pique, not the natural fade-out between people who have moved on. (Anyway, 'I've moved on' usually means 'I've abandoned someone'.) I can see the sulky look on that slightly-too-fleshy face. When Stewart and I flew home from skiing in Aus-tria and the plane circled in over the city – this was daylight so I had no shining nocturnal sweep to muse on as I had before the descent tonight – I tried to locate Govan in the shifting panorama below me, for in Govan there stood, invisible to everyone but me, a tall transmitter like in the old trademark for RKO movies. It radiated pulses of resentment in all direc-tions and our plane was just coming into receiving range.

When in the spring of 1986 an envelope arrived addressed in Robert's handwriting I took it into the lavatory to read. I locked the door, which is something Stewart and I did not normally do, though I locked it quietly so he would not know.

Dear Mark,

I hope you do'nt mind me writing, its just that I have'nt really got anyone else, all our friends are Nigels. Nigel and I seem to be falling apart, just my luck.

Oh, the fatalism of the boy from Govan who doesn't think things can ever go right for him!

> I get pretty depressed. I think of all the other mistakes I made.

> But *he* hasn't made any.

> Nigel wants this David to come and live with us, he say's hes just a lodger, but I know better. Nigel say's he needs a place to live because he went and got tested for this AIDS and something got sent to his home and his parents threw him out, allthough it was negative.

> What Im writing for is not to hassle you with my problems, I know Ive got to face them on my own, but to ask if you know anywhere I can rent to live, cheap?

> Hoping to hear from you, Robert.

There are plenty of shop windows that carry cards advertising flats. What he is really asking is: am I free, can we be lovers?

I replied:

> Dear Robert,

> Sorry to hear about your problems. I'm afraid I don't know of anyone with a room to let.

There could be no harm in attempting a bit of comfort, in showing him that someone knew there was a fond loving heart inside the miracle of that functioning body, even if Nigel couldn't see it:

> Remember, it might be all as Nigel says, nothing to worry about. Maybe you're imagining problems where there aren't any. Romantics do that and you always were a romantic – I remember you singing 'Strangers in the Night' in 1977, the line about "in love forever". Take care, Mark.

Obviously, I couldn't end it "Yours". As compensation I went and copied down addresses from a window in Byres Road and put them with the letter.

Next Christmas he wrote in a big glittery card: "Thanks a million. Fantastic flat." The Gibson Street address was one of those I'd sent him. And the card was signed, "Robert and David" with a shameless ampersand!

The sly clever bugger! That would teach that Nigel to mess with my Robert. Yes, the phone book had a number for him at the Gibson Street flat: telephone lines ran between us. Of course, I didn't telephone.

These were years in which deaths were becoming more frequent, and when no card came in 1989, I feared the obvious. We were told we shouldn't speak of *victims* of AIDS, but poor loving Robert would have been a victim all right – victim of two-faced David's slimy infidelities. All was explained next year, though. "The business is really taking off. We spent last Christmas in the Bahamas and did'nt send a single card. Sorry!"

There was never another mention of the business, before or after. That was significant. It meant I was someone Robert's thoughts flew to at all sorts of times and junctures. He was so used to talking to me in his mind that he forgot he'd told me nothing about the business in fact.

One year his card arrived in the middle of November. This was significant too. It announced a change of address: he didn't want to risk not getting my card. It mattered to him that a card my hands had touched, signed, placed in its envelope, should cross the city and end up between his fingers.

Am I giving the impression that the years were absolutely dominated by these cards, were nothing but the before and after of exchanging cards with Robert at Christmas? Oh, no. I had a full life going on in the real world, in the daylight, in which I didn't give a thought to Robert from one year's end to the next. I left my council job and trained as a teacher, Stewart got to run a library, we lived through the Poll Tax and the Gulf War in 1991, Stewart's sister was murdered . . .

They – for it was still "Robert & David" – now lived in Kelvin Court in Great Western Road. A classy address: the business was indeed doing well. Of course, it was all Robert's doing, his drive and acumen that fired it.

One dark, rainy evening – it was the anniversary of the day Stewart and I had set up home together – I was driving home on a high of joy about my life with Stewart. I was actually smiling with the joy. I pulled into the car park at Kelvin Court. I sat there with the engine off. I looked up at the great proud 1930s blocks of flats with their jutting wings. High up inside were Robert and David. At the door would be a set of bell-pushes with illuminated frames for occupants's names. I imagined Robert's surname conjoined with another: McHugh Brodie, McHugh Jenkins, McHugh Watson. I realised these were all real Davids I had known.

I got out. At what looked like a main entrance there were numbers and bell-pushes but no frames for occupants' names. Really classy places didn't have them, I supposed. Still, I let a magnetic force draw my thumb to the right bell-push. I rested it there. My thumb pulsed with the electric connection. "Just passing, thought I'd look you up," I could say. The slightest pressure would burst me into Robert's unknown world.

But what would be the point?

There seemed to be some kind of superintendent's office adjoining the entrance, lighted. I thought I caught a movement. If someone came out and asked me my business, what could I say? So I pocketed my thumb and hurried away and drove off in the rain, and Robert would never know that I had stood there with my thumb joined to the bell-push. Things like that happen all the time in cities and no-one knows about them.

Although with Stewart I had the happiness one dreams of, nevertheless there are people who will understand how, the day after I came out from identifying his body, without waiting until Christmas, I could write:

Dear Robert,

Stewart died in a car crash.

I realise now I'd never told him I had a partner.

I've lots of people to write to, but first things first.

Clever sentence that, both ranking Robert among the lots and giving him special status.

I can't believe I'm a single man again. Perhaps you never do become single again after a deep experience of connection, no matter how long. Or short.

Through the ether I willed him to understand that.

Strange, I'm already reaching out towards the idea of a new relationship. Stupid, of course. Mark.

There was no reply until Christmas, and then the card was not in Robert's handwriting: "Tough about you and Stephen. David & Robert." I'd caused little rat-faced David to assert himself in that grand balconied flat high up in Kelvin Court: "Just an old friend, you say. Christ, he's practically begging you to go and live with him. No, *I'll* see to the card. I'm going to put a stop to this."

He did. Robert decided I must be sacrificed to protect his relationship with David and stopped sending cards – further proof of integrity, for he could have sent me cards on the sly. I did what he wanted, stopped sending to him. Until I moved away from Glasgow to a new job down in Croydon. From that distance there could be no harm in sending a card again. I didn't put my new address: that would say "Please reply" too obviously.

I did pay the Post Office to redirect my mail from my old address. And yes, Robert was sharp enough to work that out, though his card emphasised a joint tie: "Wev'e got two dogs, Posh and Ginger. Its like having kids to look after."

Next Christmas I replied jokily, "It is a truth universally acknowledged that a poof couple in a settled life must be in want of substitute kids." Of course Robert wouldn't get the literary allusion. His bombshell arrived a month later:

> You have to know that David and I have split up. He wants children and is looking for a woman to give him kids. Its a farce, she wo'nt give him anything else he wants, thats for sure, heh heh.

Not the words of someone whose life has been shattered, but a boy like Robert just doesn't have the vocabulary to express what's going on in his fond loving core.

So here I am, stepping off the 'plane, beginning the trudge along the tedious airport corridors that will lead me to – what? It strikes me that none of the beliefs I have about Robert or about anything else has the slightest power to influence what is about to happen or not happen. A bang from someone's hand-luggage informs me I've halted in my tracks.

I sent him a postcard saying, "Arriving Glasgow airport 10-15 Friday night, British Midland flight from Heathrow. Meet?" The last word could be passed off merely as a suggestion to meet for a chat during a stay in Glasgow made for other reasons.

And here is the desk, deserted at this time of night, where the corridors emerge into the public area. My eye surveys the people waiting for arrivals. They look drab and spiritless, you can't credit them with real feelings. Among them is a man in a brown suede carcoat. He's looking down, smiling secretly. Yes, he has gone bald, almost entirely so, and the hair that's left straggles over the collar. He's not tried to keep middle-age at bay by shaving it close.

Ah, but once you have loved someone, why, the person you have loved is always invisibly there. We shake hands, linking the fingers that have so often exchanged touch through Christmas cards. I do not know what to say.

I say, "So what was the business?"

I mean, what sort of business, but he thinks I am asking for the name and says, "Music Markdown". Oh, I know of it: cut-price compact discs by mail-order, run from an address on the south side. Indeed, I've bought CDs from the firm. (Correction: Stewart and I did.) So the post had woven further invisible threads between us. The order form had gone from our house to Robert's dusty office, not that he would have recognised my name. (Did the form say, in small print at the top, "Proprietor: R McHugh"? I try to call it up in my memory and look.)

He repeats his firm's name, dividing the second word into two, and I feel a great jolt of joy. He is saying: "You have to know. I was very happy with David. Until."

And I have to say, "So was I with Stewart."

We walk to the airport exit in silence but that is all right because our history has been nearly all silence. As we cross the road to the car-park all the airport lights create an unreal science-fiction landscape that has nothing to do with homely things like, oh, hair over a collar and Christmas cards and bell-pushes. The illuminated neon sign on Robert's office premises zooms upwards in the night, growing and growing until it dwarfs the city, until the whole of Glasgow is nothing but the huddled base and support for a tower of masts and props and pylons miles high which rotates a vast flashing sign, 'Mark Down'. It shines year in, year out, though the city's life goes on as it always does.

Sabhal Mór Ostaig

COLAISDE GHAIDHLIG NA h-ALBA
Scotland's Gaelic College, Isle of Skye

Short Courses

Gaelic conversation courses at all levels, Mon-Fri every week 26 June-1 September £120
Traditional music courses from £110: Fiddle, Clarsach, Gaelic Song, Accordion
Keyboard, Step-dance, Piping, Band, Flute

HIGHLAND WRITING – 7-11 August £120 **Ian Stephen, Rody Gorman** One week workshop to cover fiction and poetry in Gaelic or English New writers welcome as well as established ones

accommodation available at the College
Brochure available from: Gavin Parsons, Short Course Organiser.
Sabhal Mor Ostaig, Isle of Skye IV44 8RQ, phone 01471 888 240
Fax 01471 888 001 e-mail gavin@smo.uhi.ac.uk

Robin Hamilton

The Tenth Circle
Or/ For When the Melancholy Mood Comes On

Above was written:
    There was never hope –
We lost it long ago.

My love among the apple-blossoms
    crowned her hair with roses
Flower among such several flowers.

Summer was cruel to her,
Autumn despised her,
But both deferred to loveless Winter.

Visiting for a time,
    leaving the children,
Till the holiday ends.

Age could not break him
    nor pain disconcert
But a touch on his wrist proved the straw.

Blessed Anacreon with your spirit caught
    in a cage of bone empty of flesh,
I too endure that girl of Thrace.

Haughty, and perilous, her despite
    bought of an angel's grief:
Coy mistress of the unfulfilled.

The lunatics inhabit the asylum
    the citizens own the town:
God wonders why he bothered.

The price of sweet sin
    is to languish a mornings
Chastened by the noon sun.

Choices and prices
    better not to buy
At that shop.

There was a river once
    and a bridge –
But the floods came.

Sweet Sappho whose broken songs
    mark out her territory
Lies here alone.

Golden boys lapped
        in their toil of dreams,
The best always behind.

The girls in their petticoats
        dance beside the stream
While the stream looks on.

Too many heroes
    under one roof
And the women absent.

Apollo god of dignity
    pisses against a tree
While a satyr watches.

Sometimes life loses its worth.
        Sometimes the blood chills at memory
Until her voice drifts down the wind.

Hope and despair,
    grief and some laughter –
Life shaken not stirred.

Auburn on Blonde

Bright set my lady walked her course of grey.
"Oh for some fire from heaven to light my life,"
        she said,
Laughing at the gulls which wheeled above her.

But always the anger at that old passion,
As she shredded kerchief after kerchief
        between hands
Grown claws to tear his throat.

"Why did he, miserable sanctimonious
Compromiser that he was, and all for love
        of her blond hair –
May he rot in the garden that grips him."

So she turned blind to her futures, in a wind
Which lifted her spread hair, and the
        wind chuckled
To know he walked the other side of her hedge.

A Poem that Says It's Too Late

Let's imagine a man writing a story. He's a man at
That certain time of life when the girls look at him
Like a fond uncle you like but have to be careful with –
Too old to attract, not old enough to be neuter.
So he makes up this story about a young girl who is
Everything, and who enters his life neatly and strange
And all is smooth as expensive ice-cream. Odd
That it hurts so much more when the story is true.

Irfan Merchant

Certification

starry
eyes wide as
the black sky
have seen beyond
the stars

listen to the
emptiness
the hollow

stillness calmed
the drum of
life

even breaths
are stilled
awed

and pulseless.

We were attached
only in death

opposite ends
of a stethoscope.

Yet you know
the darkness
in my soul.

I close your case notes:

3.15 am
Called to confirm death.
No vital signs.

Violin

He said
silencing
the folk
session.

The next week
he remembered
to say
fiddle.

Cornershop

They sell all sorts:
right angles
curves
thirty degrees, sixty degrees

And if they
haven't got one
in stock
they will order it
for you.

Asylum seeker

It is a demonstration
that the system works
said the prison service

when Enahoro Esemuze
wrapped a strip of blanket
around his throat

and hung his scarred
Nigerian body
in his detention cell.

He was spotted
before he harmed himself
seriously

said the prison service.

Spikken The Hert

Aimée Chalmers

Learnin The Guid Book

A wis the wee een, the shakkins o the poke.

Ma faither nivver hid much tae say tae me, jist, "Awa an git ma fags!" an oan a Seterday nicht ee'd say "fars ma pincil?" an "haud yer tung!" fan the fitba scores come oan the wireless.

"Arbroath 3, MOntrose 1. FOrfAr 7, BrETCHin, Nil"

Thon mannie c'dna sae the Scots nims tae save eesell. MOntrose, FOrfAr, BrETCHin. Specially BrETCHin, ee aye made an erse o't.

Fit a lauch, bit ye'd tae lauch ahent yir haun, sae's ye didnae mak a noise n git yer faither riled.

"Get oot o' that!" ee sais tae me fan A wint intae ees baderoom ae Sunday moarnin an spiered if ma mither winted a cuppie tea. "Go'an, get oot o that!"

She sais she'd hae een in a minitie. Bit ee nivver winted een.

Ma faither aye spoke the same wiy, in Scots, faa'iver ee wis spikken tae.

Bit ma mither c'd spikk Scots, an poash Ingilish fan she winted, tae the meenister an the teacher an the doacter, fowk like at. Fan she pit oan er guid claes, er moo wint a different shipp, mair pu'ed in like, an er tung wabbled aboot a different wiy.

Fan ye wisna weel ye goat tae lie in her bed, wi the firie oan, waitin fir the Doactor.

An if she wis spikken aboot the doactor, she'd draa er chin in an shak er heid fae side tae side like a waably doag.

"The Doactor said . . ." An, "wheesht, wheesht, wheesht . . ." Ye didnae sae it loud, fit the doactor said.

Sae that's foo A learnt the Ingilish, fae ma mither. It wis fir yasin wi the fowk thit tellt ye fit tae dae. An it wisnae jist a wiy o spikken, ye wirna the same bodie, ye wir different yersell fan ye yased that langwidge.

Then it the schule ye learnt thit it wisna jist different wiys o spicken, ae wiy wis richt an ae wiy wis wrang. Their wiy wis richt, an oor wiy wis wrang.

In the playgrun ye cried, "Gies the baa! Gies the baa!"

Bit ye'd tae lave they wirds ootside, wi the baas, fan ye wint in agin.

Sae ye learnt tae sae the wirds the wiy the teacher winted. Nae muckle wunner. Yon buik, *First Aid in English* – jees, ye'd tae ken yon buik aff bi hert.

At buik mad we hink Ingilish wis oor langwidge.

"The English language . . . is one of the most progressive of modern languages . . . many words now in common use . . . have their origin in such languages as Latin, Greek, French, Dutch and German."

Oh weel then, that wis us pit in oor pliss. Nae Scoats wirds ava.

An b'Goad, bi the time we goat tae page 83, we sh'd've kent fine the answer tae the question, "Explain meaning of a 'dead' language."

Bit jist tae mak share, oan page 88, we wis tellt, an nae mistaak. Scotland wis there, bit the langwidge we spoke wis English ir Gaelic. Nae Scoats avaa.

The female negro m'be wisna affa plaised tae be caaed a negress, and er bairn a picaninny. Bit it least they wis there.

There wis nae mannies ir wifies ir bairnies ava.

Mibbe it wis worth learnin aboot "a baren of mules, a covert of coots, a clowder of cats, a rag of colts an a smuck of jellyfish".

Aither that ir oor teachers wis a richt "pace of asses" fir fillen up oor heids wi that havers.

Ach, as fir me, A wisna bathered, A c'd spick Ingilish tae the teachers if that wis fit they winted. A learned the buik like A wis tellt.

Bit A wis aye cumfier spikken tae the Jannie.

Spikken the Hert

A wint tae wirk fir the Cooncil, i the heid bummer's oaffice, tae see 'Fair Do's!' fir aabodie.

Ye'd tae mind fa ye wis spikken tae, ir the cooncillirs micht tak the huff.

A goat affa guid it scrievin reports wi'oot saein oanyhin rilly. An nae saein hings it mettered. Aa in best committee . . . *First Aid in English*. It'd cum in handy efter aa.

There wis hings ye didnae wint the cooncillirs tae ken, an hings ye wished they did ken, but ye c'dna say.

"No, take that out. You can't say that in a report."

Ye 'assess the situation' and 'quantify the problem' involving 'identification of priorities'. Then, after 'facilitating appropriate consultation' investigate whether 'within available resources' there can be 'consideration given to' . . . 'liason' or better still 'partnership' with the 'voluntary sector'.

Perhaps with a view to 'formulate a policy'?

An of coorse, ye've tae 'disseminate the results' iv yer spierin.

Eence ye kent the richt wiy o daein, ye c'd write a report oan oanything. As lang as ye jist spikk fae yer heid.

Tae pit it anither wiy, d'e *commit* yersell, cis if ye dae the cooncil'll hae tae yase money it hisnae goat. (Ye'll git awa wi't as lang as ye wear a suit an a tie, an say it in Ingilish.)

Enough wis enough.

A wrote doon a wee stoary o ma ain.

M'be ill hung the gither, bit ma stoary . . . in Ingilish, iv coorse.

A thocht a'd feenished 't, bit fit wid ye ken, ma faither cam alang an pit eesell in't, spickin in Scots.

A wis fair dumfoonered. Ee wis lang deed, ye ken.

A stairted anither een. Mibbe A c'd write a Scots wird here an there. Safe enough tae say 'brig n bonnie'. Aabody kens they wirds.

Bit 'ken' wis 'know', an a 'palaver' wis still a 'fuss' .

Then it started A heard the soond o Scots in ma heid.

Waak'nin up i the moarnin, sittin oan the lavvy pan, oanypliss, A'd hink o wirds A hadna heard fir a lang time.

It wis fell hard tae spell they wirds. A'd nivver learnt tae write Scots. An oanywiy, the wiy A spoke wisnae rilly Scots, wis it?

There'd likely be a richt wiy, nae my wiy.

A spiered, "How do you spell pliss? Is it flooers or flouers?"

A goat aa raivelled.

A wrote 'whaur? an wha', wirds a'd seen written doon. Bit in Mintrose we sais 'Far? n Fa?'.

"Far ye gaain?" "Foo far?" "Fa is?" "Fan?"

Wis it aa richt tae write at doon?

Punctuashin wis a scunner. Apostrophies aa ower the pliss. A didnae wint naebodie tae hink A wis igirant.

Then A saa a wee book aboot Scots. A wint fae cover tae cover as if A wis lickin a plitt o Cura's ice cream.

Scots isna bad English ava, it sais! It's a langwidge! They're richt words! They dinna need nae apostrophies!

A wis that plaised A c'd've grat. A flung aa they apostrophes awa.

It turned oot the stoary A wis scrieven wisnae aboot a brig ava – it wis aboot ma faither. An aa iv a sudden A kent fit tae say.

A'd nivver rilly spoke tae ma faither. Nae mair'n A hid tae.

"Here's yer fags. Dae ye wint yer tea afore the fitba scores?"

Bit noo, fir the first time, A wis spikken tae'm. The wirds cam richt oot ma hert. Scots wirds. Fit wis ees langwidge an culcher wis ma langwidge an culcher an aa.

Nae mair ma tung wabblin aboot in ma moo, it's root loast. Fir noo it's fund, an it gaes a the wiy doon tae ma hert.

A'll nae haud ma wheesht nae mair, nae fir naebody.

The Dying Art of Seaside Towns

Roddy Hamilton

The woman was in her fifties. She wore a beige blouse and patterned, mainly terracotta scarf and pleated cotton trousers. She stood in the large doorway of one of the seafront guesthouses – one of the many which face Memorial Park and the beach and whose names are etched in bronze plaques or painted in primary colours on varnished wood by their doors – names like Seaview, Beachview and Parkview Hotel – names that are united in their lack of individuality.

The dog which she kept closely to heel was black, possibly a labrador or similar, and young, you would judge by its rascally behaviour, although not still a puppy.

Behind the woman and behind the open door was another door, this one made predominantly of stained glass and with a large brass door-knob. This the woman pulled closed behind her while the dog jumped up excitedly and placed its front paws on her cotton trousers at the knee. The woman seemed to say something to the dog and promptly it sat, with a reluctant sort of obedience, onto the tiles in the small shadowy hallway. The woman looked out through the exterior door to the brightness outside (it was early evening and the sun was lower than it had been but still strong). She opened a small leather shoulder bag. Across the road on the edge of the park she could see the signs that, every twenty yards or so, read *No Dogs Allowed.* She breathed a sigh which was immediately stolen by the breeze.

The bunched folds of the dog lead in her hand hampered her immediate access to the bag. She had to take out a couple of smaller items before she could find what she wanted – a black leather pouch containing sunglasses with pink-tinted lenses – which she immediately put on and then ran her fingers through her hair.

On either side of her were the small, neat gardens of the neighbouring guesthouses. Here each rockery had the same hydrangeas and marigolds and a few further up had painted clay gnomes and one even a plastic model wishing well. White signs stood in a line, garden after garden, like flattened bird boxes, the legend *No Vacancies* written on each – at least the ones she could see. Why then, the woman found herself wondering, was it so quiet. All day she'd hardly seen a soul.

Memorial Park, an oblong patch of undulating grass around the size of four abutting football pitches is bisected in the middle by a concrete path which runs from the guesthouses on one side, in a straight line and right through to the beach esplanade. Half way along its length, this path opens out to house the centrepiece of the park; the eponymous memorial, fifty-three feet of sandstone obelisk, tiered, like the upturned shaft of a telescope, and with the names of the war-dead carved into it with solemnity, dedication and respect.

The woman with the black dog began to walk around the perimeter of the park and turned right at its corner, walking parallel with the sandy beach. She heard the noise of the waves, a distance away, over the sea wall. She kept a tight leash on the dog, which weaved this way and that so that she had to constantly change the lead from hand to hand. The salt breeze cooled her face. Sand gathered and dispersed at the base of the sea wall.

After a short while, she had walked more than a half way round. She was standing at the third corner of the park, about to turn back towards the row of guesthouses on the street when she saw someone in the near distance. She found it surprising that she should see anyone at all (the park had been empty for most of the day) but more surprising was the fact that she recognised the approaching figure as that of the lady guesthouse owner, bent over a little, with a headscarf held down by her hand although the light sea breeze by no means required it.

"A pleasant evening," she prepared herself to say to the guesthouse owner; and perhaps she would have been brave enough also to wonder out loud, "where *is* everyone?" but she didn't, in fact had no time to, before the guesthouse owner rushed right past her, looking straight ahead through those bifocals of hers which weren't bifocals at all but spectacle frames with half lenses in the bottom half and nothing, not even glass, in the top half.

Around five minutes later, the woman was almost back outside the guest house. Beside her was one of the signs which ran all around the park and read, *No Dogs Allowed*. The woman looked around her then seemed to glance at her watch. She paused for several minutes, took her sunglasses off, then put them on again. She ran her fingers through her hair. She shuffled to face this way then that along the road. Nothing. No cars, even. She could not think of a single summer when this place had appeared so empty.

The woman stood on the pavement by the sign and slid the loop of the dog leash over one hand. From the shoulder bag she took some lipstick. She took off the lid, wound up a bullet of colour and, using the sunglasses as a tiny mirror, she covered first her bottom lip then her top lip.

The dog sat beneath her while this went on, its pink tongue hung loose from its jaws, quivering as it panted in the warmth. The woman crouched down to the dog, clapped it. The dog panted harder. The woman took the lead and wrapped it round the *No Dogs Allowed* sign. She wound it round two, possibly three times, then turned the end of it through on itself and secured it with a sharp tug. The dog bowed its head. Its tail stopped wagging. The woman held her forefinger up to her lips then pointed at the dog's nose. The dog sniffed. It seemed to understand. It sat down and shuffled its front paws. As the woman walked away, its ears twitched at the disappearing sound of her feet on the grass.

The woman did not want to turn, did not want to acknowledge the dog in any way, in case it became restless and fought against its lead to follow her, but after a suitable distance she *did* look round, although didn't stop, and only a second later faced forward again.

A slow but deliberate walk took her towards the memorial, with the concrete path a little to her left. The grass was hilly as it had always been. Sometimes she thought she could recall from her childhood the geography of this or that dip or shallow, or this or that ridge or valley, and from this feeling of *deja-vu* she could conjure up the oblique fragments of memories; a bird in the sky became a kite, for one fleeting moment so real that she turned to look around for the child clutching the kitestrings. And once, as she upturned her face to the lowering sun, she realised that the ticklish wetness on her face wasn't spilt ice-cream, only tears brought on by the salt air on her eyes.

Closer up she saw that the rain had over the years blurred the incisions of the mason's chisel. Sandstone is a porous rock. Up close it can look like a sponge. The names on the memorial were all still clearly visible, but the characters of the words were shallower now – rounded and less distinct than they once were.

She traced some of these names with a fingertip. Her eyebrow touched the monument's edge. She smelled grass-pollen, exhaust-fumes and salt in the red stone. In the past she was sure it had been only warmth and coal-smoke she'd smelled, but that had been a long time ago in a busier, halcyon succession of bright summers. She wondered where those summers had gone, felt sad that they should disappear without proper warning or regard to nostalgia. She closed her eyes and heard children playing, the sharp crack of cricket ball on bat, ting of tennis ball on string, feet running on these hollow grass mounds, heavy breathing, distant screaming, a Punch 'n' Judy show. And there was the beach train's dirty engine, the splash of its coloured body snaking in and out of the waves, her grandfather's voice as deep and sure and rich with history as the monument.

Down the concrete stairs and step back onto the grass.

Here, she re-tied the terracotta scarf. She ran her fingers through her hair, sensing the dust from the sandstone still under her nails. Almost completely in the centre of the park now, she wondered whether to take the path or wander back over the empty blanket of grass. She stopped to consider this, and looked over to the row of guesthouses. The sun was low above the sea behind her, beginning to stoke a fire on the waves and, as she began across the grass, the windows of the houses exploded in light as though a row of mirrors were arranged there instead. Her sinewy shadow stretched long in front of her. The park seemed suddenly to be more expansive than her memory reminded her it had been. When she cupped a hand above her eyes she could discern the numerous outlines of the signs, equally spaced at the far edge of the park, but much further away than she had expected; and beneath one of them – the proper one

– she could see that the dog was safe and sound.

She set off towards it, imagining its wagging tail, its gladness at her return, when something caught her eye. Another sign, this time in the middle of the park – set low in one of the many small depressions – peculiar and vulgar to be stuck there in an area of calm. It did not face her, the sign, but looked away from her, towards the guest houses, as if in a sulk.

The woman descended the grassy hillock, having at once to slow herself by putting all her weight on each new footstep and yet to keep the momentum going so as not to stop completely and overbalance backwards. From all the times she'd visited the park as a child she could not remember this part. The geography of it did not seem familiar at all; and when at last she reached the bottom, where the tall sign was implanted in the grass, the sun had almost disappeared behind her, behind the hill; and in the dimness, despite her close proximity to it, she had to squint to read the sign and mouthed the words as she read them; *KEEP OFF THE GRASS*.

T S Law: A Generous Anger

Tom Hubbard

Introducing Tom Law's debut collection, *Whit Tyme In The Day* (1948), Hugh MacDiarmid stressed Law's firmly Scottish intellectualism, praising the "half-hints, fragmentary suggestions, subtle allusions" to be found throughout. By day, Law was variously an aircraft fitter, miner, technical writer: the ideal example for MacDiarmid's insistence that, with their traditional strengths in technology and science, hardheaded Scots ought to be resistant to the sentimental inanities that had so often vitiated their culture. Law "mixed mind with his material".

Yet in childhood and early adolescence, by his own admission, Law "showed little scholarly ability and less interest in fostering such a thing". He had no university education. In spite, or even because of that, his poetry is among the most intellectual (as distinct from academic) composed in Scotland this century. Here he is perhaps matched only by Mac-Diarmid, sharing his Faustianly voracious appetite for knowledge and analysis, counterpointed by an awareness of the mind's limitations:

> No sic a gomeril as tae say muckle aboot
> whit he didnae ken, but wyss enyeuch athoot
> kennin whye he did, he badd his wheesht tae listen.
> His wyssheid cawed gy caunnie wi self-doot . . .

> ('A Philosophie', in New Poetry, Spring 1980)

This echoes MacDiarmid's Drunk Man: "I lauch to see my crazy little brain/ . . . tak'n itsel' seriously".

Law's poetry is intensely dialectical. He delights, again like MacDiarmid, in the juxtaposition of opposites, "as tho delyte made guid-desyre delytit the-wy desyre maks-guid delyte desyrous" (*Wilderness*, unpublished typescript dated 1986). Juxtaposition implies conflict; Law is not squeamish anent public tensions as fit matter for his art. He does not so much bring politics into poetry as bring poetry into politics. While politically well to the left, Law is an artist suspicious of dogmatism, whatever its source:

> Depressed by the spurious in literature,
> the alter ego images of the litterateurs,
> time servers of conservative convention,
> I look at those other alter-egos, the (Party) line-shooters
> who have nothing to say but keep on marking time,
> an establishment of rub-a-dub-dub already
> in disestablishment – so earnest those latter,
> so god-awful earnest, so god-awful depressing
> except in their own assessing.
> Better the former, better by far the old convention
> of form and subject when accepted for love,
> like the summer air singing through the strings of the trees,
> not duty like a banner above the brass
> on a cold October day with the threat of snow.
> Better by far, for it stands up to every test
> but personal dislike, the best.

('The Big Drum of Socialist Realism', *Voices of Dissent*, ed. Farquhar McLay)

His contempt for what he called "Cannae Scots" is formidable even to those who share his outlook. We've become lulled by PC euphemism, but here's a poet who won't suffer fusionless fools gladly. His idiom owes much to isolation, even at times despair; one thinks of MacDiarmid in Whalsay during the 1930s. Law shares the lonely integrity of his *Moses at Mount Sinai* (excerpts in *Cencrastus*, Spring 1985), refusing to yield to the Golden Calf. He is the poet-as-prophet, much too stern for the tastes of latter-day Aarons and their followers. Yet the dialectic, as ever, is in operation: there is simply so much of his *oeuvre* that yields great pleasure. He is the quintessentially Scottish blend of puritan and sensualist. Among living Scottish poets, Esperantist Bill Auld is the one to whom we might most readily relate Tom Law. Auld, too, is a rigorous intellectual in the Scottish tradition; if Law brings poetry into politics, Auld brings poetry into sex, and his own English translation of his *The Infant Race* (excerpts in *The Scottish Review*, Aug and Dec 1980) is a tour-de-force at once thoughtful and erotic. Both poets offer a poetry of abundance: "Here there are little cheeses dried out in rushy baskets,/ plums that are getting ripe in the sultry autumn weather,/ nuts from the chestnut tree and the red panache of apples:/ here is the kingdom of Ceres, and Bacchus, and Cupid the young" (Auld). Ceres: name of both the pagan goddess of agriculture, and of a beautiful Fife village, situated in lush farmland. This is Law again:

> Here, girl, and there and yonder with a helix wynd,
> The king of all the swallows slices yon slithering waver
> Of a mavis' song; surely your hair is harp strings
> Twanging to the birling of a wing, the singing
> Of spray from an overhead brown arm through clear green water.
>
> I would have the sun itself a melody of peach
> And pomegranate for your hair, poem of the tingling light,
> But your eyes are splintering a sea of gray and green song,
> See, here and now and into the sharps of movement along
> The air preening swallows' wings
> To a world that sings beyond your hair the matter
> Of keeping to the black keys to make a Scottish song, O golden daughter.
>
> ('Ceres, Scotland', in *Whit Tyme in the Day*)

Read any Scots-language poem by T S Law and you are soon aware of his debt to the mediaeval makars, particularly his beloved Henrysoun's *The Testament of Cresseid*. This is evident not only in linguistic idiom but also in subject matter: he echoes both Henrysoun's judgement on *vanitas vanitum* and his sensuous celebration of a Scottish ingle-neuk in winter, when one settles down with a book and a dram.

"Contrair qualities": MacDiarmid's phrase, but there we have T S Law. In 1987 Joy Hendry cited his "fusion of our oral and literary traditions", which have all too often been separated by snobbery (including inverted) Law wrote lyrics for the protest songs of the anti-Polaris movement, and indeed music itself is a favourite subject in his poetry; the dialectical poet is a contrapuntalist in words. His most pervasive references to folk idiom are to children's games, of which his knowledge was encyclopaedic. He loved children, and his gentle side is at its most appealing in this sonnet:

Man, it was an awfielik slaister o troke i the gairden the-day,
auld tin cans, a rickle o sticks, an yle-drum, pats
an pans, and a fankle o cavie wire lik the turrivees
o a surrealist gane wuid wi a bunnetfou o bees
hotterin ower the byke o his brain. "Noo, whit did ye say
that is son?" said I tae the young engineer. "Oh, that's
a rocket, daddie" said the bairn wi een lik the fuhll
muin. Truith, but lukin at him, ma ain een were gyan dull.

Raxin for the starns, it's caad, the same auld stent
ilk generatioun had wrocht wi its pickle mair,
faither tae son, and i the end faur less nor was kent
o the starns his mither fund and I, whan thare
was wunder atween us lik the muin tae pree,
gy lik the wunder in oor laddie's ee.

(The Rocket', in *Aftentymes a Tinkler,* 1975)

Law both honours and embodies "Scots casual kindlinesses". Near the end of his fiercely political piece 'Abbey Craig tae Stirlin Castle' he records a young girl's request that he sign her copy of his anthology *Homage To John MacLean* (1973). Law affectionately obliges, then offers her a verse bearing the line: "an mynd that Scotland's guid gaes weel wi grace."

I don't believe that, for this poet of 'commitment', Scotland was ever an abstraction. He knew who he was fighting for. Angry he was, yes, but as Orwell said of Dickens, he was "generously angry". In a 1987 letter to me he referred to "the common man in the common place saying the uncommon thing." That is the point, and counterpoint, of Tom Law himself.

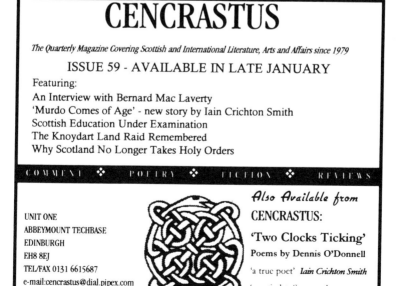

T S Law: A Life o Makkin

John Law

RAF days an *Whit Tyme in the Day*

Born Newarthill, 1916, the evidence o ma faither's life as a workin poet begins on RAF notebeuks datit 1942, Africa, whaur he wis postit as an airframe fitter. Twa things (we hae ti jalouse) actit thegither in thae war years, on tap o his lang habit o wide readin, ti gar him stert. He haed met an faan in love wi ma mither, an event that pit peyed ti an aerlier, unhappy mairiage we niver haerd muckle aboot; an he haed made ane of his key lifelang freins in the Welshman Cornelius Murphy, RAF corporal ti Jock Law's sergeant – an o coorse, as the RAF made Jock o Tam Law, it made Paddy oot o Conn Murphy for aa his Welshness, an Jock an Paddy thay badd aa thair days in amang the faimlie.

The pseudonym TSL first thocht on uisin stertin oot ti publish his wark wis *Thrawn*, an he uised this for whit we think micht be his first published poem in a Sooth African paper at haes (for nou) hidden itsel ower again amang the files. He haed a nem for thrawn in the faimlie, an he keepit that I can tell ye. The darg begins wi poems in Inglis, but bi 1944 he wis stertin uisin Scots, an he wrate in the baith languages aa his days, tho faur mair in Scots gin ye lae oot o accoont twa-three langer Inglis warks. Bi the end o the war an comin back hame, he seems ti hae been mair or less fullie-formed as a poet, an ti hiv yokit the Renaissance programme ti his ain ends.

Whit wey sae monie o the postwar makars sprang oot the forces ready-made Scots nationalists an socialist republicans I canna richtlie tell ye – the war experience claerlie made Brits oot o ithers involved. Nae dout it's got something ti dae wi the Scots ingyne (whaur present) an its closer scrutiny o the officiar clesses o the Empire an the Empire itsel in thae years. Thare is the gigantic feigur o MacDiarmid ti conseider an aa: his influence on younger bards. I ken at baith thae things haed thair influence on T S Law.

Hamish Henderson in his smaa-magazine journalism o the late 40s mentions T S Law's wark in a nummer o reviews o Scots letters, as for example in this frae *Conflict* in Mairch 1949:

> The Fife miner, T S Law, has also eschewed short cuts and has not been afraid in his first book *Whit Tyme in the Day* to grapple in the grand manner with the massy Scots tradition. Poems in this book such as 'The Clenched Fist' mark a formidable achievement . . .

This poem at Hamish Henderson admired in *Whit Tyme in the Day* is a gey deificult ane, an TSL haes a nem for bein a deificult poet at uises a deificult Scots embeddit in a deificult gremmar. Wi the owerview o the hail lifework afore me nou, I dout sic a view isna weel justifee'd avaa.

But whiles it's the speed an reinge o his thocht at maks for ae kinna deificultie: it's haurd ti jalouse ti some poems hit ye juist hou faur he's takkin ye. Conseider the poem 'Hungers', at first sicht juist an ingenious leet o kyns o hungirs; syne think hou the moral trajectory o the poem taks ye frae innocent appetite throu temptation, sin an despair ti the grave in ae bite!

Dunfaurline

In the late 40s, thae efter-war years whan thare wis aa kyns o interestin things in the warld o letters gaun forrit in Embro, TSL, efter sindrie darg cuttin peats, daein his baurman doun in Lunnon (whaur, his brithers attestit, he cut a feigur o the dourest baurman iver at sairved a pint) wis in the Peewheep an the Lindsay pits, an mibbie the Francis. He correspondit wi aa the main feigurs o the Scots Renaissance, but niver haed muckle time, siller or inclination ti hing aboot in baurs wi them.

Sax year haed gane by, frae the time he haed met Peggy MacPhail. His state o mynd, sailin awa frae Table Bay ti get feinished wi the smaa problem o Adolf Hitler, is expressed in the fine lyric, 'Table Bay', at ma faither sang ti 'Cailein Mo Runsa'; tho Tich Frier (at sings it weel on the *Scotsoun* Makars tape o T S Law's poems) thocht it wad better fit wi 'Farewell to Fiunary'.

The feelin wis mutual an strang eneuch that ma mither boardit ship her lane in 1947 ti jyne him, an thay haed a lovin mairiage at his ain poetry comments an touches on year bi the passin year. They set up hoose in Dunfaurline – whaur yer informant pit in a first appearance in 1951. This wis the time whan ma faither feinished a nummer o owersets frae the wark o Uys Krige, the Afrikaans poet, includin 'The Sodger', hereprentit. Uys Krige veisitit wi us, an thocht highly o thir owersets, peyin the compliment anent ane o them at it wis an impruvement ower his oreiginal.

Sae thare wis TSL, published, mairiet, but doun the pit. An by heckie, he didna like it. But we hae three great lang poems arisin frae this an frae ither faimlie experience o haein *wrocht at the wark*, as the sayin rins amang miners: 'Elegy for an Auld Collier', 'A Daurk Line o Fir Trees', an 'Licht Attoore the Face'. At this time tae, we hae the first evidence o contact wi Morris Blythman, the saicont o ma faither's three great freins for colloguin anent poetry an politics, a cheil at supportit, encouraged an stimulatit him aa his days. A fair wheen thay wrocht thegither ti help an brek the pouer o the Union in the Scottish mind. Ti ma young sel veisitin Morris's hoose at Rouken Glen in the Saxties, Morris wad explain things this kinna wey: "Your father is the poet of Scottish sub-cultures, John!" an hae a pul at his wee ceigar. An the pair o them wad be inti some analysis o Orange sangs, the re-modellin an subversion o these bein ane o the ploys o the time.

East Kilbride

Efter a pit accident ma faither suffert, Paddy Murphy pit in the guid word for TSL's skeel in letters an got him a stert at Napier's in Embro as a technical writer, traivellin the gate wad see him oot the lave o his aernin career at Rolls-Royce in East Kilbride. Somewhaur in ma aerlie years we'd a few month bydin doun in Richmond. I canna mynd the reasons for this faimlie muve – I jalouse mibbie job trainin ti dae wi the technical writin.

We hae ti jalouse at TSL's interest in that wark wis neist ti nane, bi his general silence on whit he did. Whit he wantit ti dae, an did dae aa the spare minutes, wis dae awa at his poetry. Efter a lenthie veisit ti Sooth Africa at he niver came on, we cam back ti the hoose at 17 Simpson Drive in East Kilbride in 1955, at he haed muved til while we war awa.

Durin aa the years ti we left East Kilbride, TSL's ootpit o poetry wis minor *in quantity*, compared ti whit gaed afore, an cam efter. I think at ma brither an masel wis mibbie ti blame for this: he pit a gey lot inti lairnin us monie a thing. But yet he wrocht awa, an monie o the tichtlie-craftit pieces o this mid-period rank amang his best: monie sonnets at he published later in the twa sonnet collections *Aftentymes a Tinkler* an *Whyles a Targe*.

The Maurlage

We muved oot ti the Maurlage near Stonehoose aboot 1962, whan a legacy frae the faimlie in Sooth Africa permittit the biggin o a hoose, Blackwood Cottage, on the site o an auld miner's raw. This hoose haed a practical an linguistic importance. It haed a separate study, its surroondins wis bonnie, whit wi ma mither's eydent wark at its gairden, an it wis Scots-speakin in a wey East Kilbride niver wis in its new toun youthheid, wi young ex-forces faimlies tendin ti uise lingua franca Inglis. The last crottles o Lanarkshire coal wis bein worked oot yet. Thare wis a drift mine three-fower fields frae us doun the road, at did awa til thay cam ower near the surface ti the burn at the fuit o oor gairden an fluidit it oot.

In 1959 at East Kilbride TSL begoud but didna feinish at that time a lang poem cried 'Moses at Mount Sinai'. It is wi the kythin o this poem we see the feinish o a lang saicont apprenticeship I think ma faither haed pitten himsel til throu thae leaner 50s years. We nou see the mainer an the subject-maiter o the mature poet. Efter this, stimulatit ti a poetry o anti-nuclear activism bi his wark alangside Morris Blythman in the Ban Polaris campaign, an wi the inspirational muve ti the Maurlage, back amang Scots-spaekin fowk, the pace o his production an publication acceleratit.

Anither major poem feinished at the Maurlage wis 'Licht Attoore the Face', at daels wi the daith o former pit neibors killt in the Lindsay Colliery disaster o 1957 lairned aboot in a newspaper he fand lyin in the road. The poem teuk its time ti growe efterhaun. Its main composeition seems ti hae taen place frae 1966-68. Apairt frae its elegaic content, evokin the struissle o pit wark, it daels wi the embattlement o the Scots workin cless an the tocher o language an Scots culture thir fowk hains fornent capitalist imperialism, fornent darg, injustice an daith. T S Law coonter-poses the eimage o himsel, as he says, "makar amang myners, but minor amang myners", tyauvin awa at the auld Scots leid for ti collier oot the seams o poetry intil't:

> But here I'm lyin-on yit, still tyauvin
> amang thir coals o the auld Scots tongue
> for aa the wurld lik an A an B
> Fifteen or Mavor an Coulson Samson
> gurriein awo at the Diamont or Glessee coals.

'Moses at Mount Sinai' is a lang poem o some fower hunder an seventie lines – short bi TSL staundarts – a moral an poleitical debate atween Aaron an Moses, anent whit's ti be thocht on the situation o Israel, nou at the Lord haes taen a haun an leuks like ti gie the chuisen fowk a heize wi it. It unlocks pairts o his complicatit poleitical an moral message.

Getherin strenth aa throu the 60s in Scotland, as aabodie kens nou, wis a new generation o Scots rebels against the Union. Sae strang wis this geth-erin force bi the hin-end o thon decade at it pit Winnie Ewing inti Parlia-ment, but it wis expressin itsel furth o the SNP an aa, on the Scottish Left.

Wi Morris Blythman an ithers, T S Law foonded the John MacLean Soci-ety, an thay editit *The Socialist Poems of Hugh MacDiarmid*, an published *Homage to John MacLean*. Juist as aerlier thay haed uised Orange tunes ti subvert loyalism in the Ban Polaris, Bay o Pigs time, sae nou thay war tyauvin awa at the MacLean-MacDiarmid strategy ti caw the Scottish Left inti support o the national struissle, or keep it rinnin true alang that dreel.

In spite o a guid record o publication in smaa journals throu the 60s an 70s, he despaired o iver finndin a commercial publisher, an he self-pub-lished a series o beuklets unner the Fingerpost imprint in the 70s: *Abbey Craig tae Stirlin Castle, Aftentymes a Tinkler, Whyles a Targe, The N C O s* an *A Pryle o Aces*. The Fingerpost ye'll can see yet: it's the auldfarrant road sign at the fit o the road frae the Maurlage ti whaur the back road we badd on jynes the Netherburn-Ashgill main road whaur he cotch his bus for East Kilbride. This road an thae bus journeys wis composeition an readin time ti him, an he wis weel-kent wi neibors oot on the road the same times for challengin the laverocks wi sangs an recites as he walked that hauf-mile.

The struissle o the '79 Referendum an follaein led ti some o T S Law's sherpest an sairest polemic at wis published in the beuk o that nem in the late 80s, wi a companion polemic anent the fate o the Heilans, *The Clear-ances*. His further wark on MacDiarmid is in the lang poem 'A Brawlik Makar', an the further warkin oot o his ain poleitical thocht in 'Freedom at Large an Quo Stalin on Lenin', the latter a Scots owerset o an orra wark o Soviet hagiography consistin o speeches bi Stalin on the subject o Lenin. The former is a lang wark explorin concepts o freedom, the latter a self-generatin satire on a model o socialism at cuidna be lippent on, written in eichtie-seiven, twa year afore the hoose o cairds blew doun its lane.

Auchterarder

Efter retirement in 1981, in '83 or '84 he wis victim o hamesucken, whan he wis set on in the Maurlage ae nicht thare his lane bi twa hoosebrekkers. Strictly speakin, he wis owercome bi them follaein an aamichtie fecht efter he jumped the ane afore finndin oot thare wis anither bastart alang wi him. Thay blinnd-fauldit him an pykit him in the back wi a screwdriver ti gar him lat on whaur wis the valuables, an thay staw an auld watch at's the subject o ae poem, an a Tay Pearl brooch at its replacement's anither.

This, an the gairden bein ower muckle for them nou thay war aulder, led ti the final muve ti Auchterarder in 1985. T S Law wis 69, but wi nae notion o packin in. Indaed, he packed in ti his neist 12 years a guid dael o darg, some o it, indaed muckle o it fair monumental in ambeition, scale an achievement. He muved I'm shuir deleiberatelie frae ticht ti lowsser screivin, ti get sayed aa whit he weished ti say nou time pressed on him.

The Magical Well wis the first muckle project he gat yokit til, a verse re-wark o a failed prose piece daelin wi the kennlin relationship atween a man an wumman nae unlike himsel an ma mither in a wey: the man,

Stephen, in this fiction haein an awfu lot ti say for himsel, excusably, bein a poet, strangely eneuch! It's a sair lenth, nae wey publishable as it stauns, but fu o guid bits. 'Quo Stalin on Lenin' an 'Freedom at Large' cam neist.

'Yeegie Landscapes' wis the neist major project. Here again, the text is sae ower-lang at it cuidna be published, but in this case the lenth is caused bi lang owersets at the end o his faither's Orange Lodge an Ryal Airch Masons haunbeuks inti Scots: duin for pleisure in the daein an somewhit oot the wey o the main intent o the lave o the text.

Aerlie Days an Late

A wheen o the makkins frae the last years o his life caa back til sic aerlie inspirations, an gif we ar ti follae time's arra wi TSL's life, we hae ti gang ti thir late poems ti see whaur the flane wis airtit. Baith 'Yeegie Landscapes' an 'An In-Memoriam' is ruitit in young Tam's life as a member o the Law faimlie in Newarthill, comin ti poetic an political consciousness thare, ten year auld in the year '26 o the General Strike. 'Yeegie Landscapes' daels wi the backgrund o cultural consciousness.

Thare is nocht else I ken o in Scottish letters peels wi 'Yeegie Landscapes' – it gies a pictur o bairntyme education, influence an fowk-laer in a Twinties minin village, ful o evocative detail o faimlie an local worthies, but is at the same time a makar's hinsicht on his ain brocht-upness, shawin us whit wey the music o words an the aerlie lessons o life airtit him the gate he'd gang. Efter this, he wrocht mainly at continuin wark weel-forrit areadies reddin aerlier maiter inti collections at's sib bi theme or bi form. Maist o thir wad mak slim or fatter volumes thairsel: *99 Novenaries, 100 Novenaries, A Birss o Jaggies, Conversaziones, Military Option, The Anti-Polaris Guitar, Uys Krige owersets, Wilderness, Light & Shade Like Sound and Silence, Extrapolations* an mair: monie's a poem at stauns its lane an didna finnd hame in a collection; the ootpit o fifty year an mair o tentie wark.

Frae 1994 on, he yieldit ti my lang threipin at he shuid uise a computer, an as he cuidna be fashed lairnin richt whit wey ti uise multiple files, he got me ti set up ae file for him every sae aften, and kept addin on his occasional poems til it, (for he niver got duin makkin them on his stocks o filin cairds wi his stubs o peencils at war the pootch graith o his ilka jaiket) ti the file got that ful the computer wis aboot founert ladin it inti memory, an he wad speir at me for ti apen anither ane. Sae in that lest three year o his life we hae three poetry files rinnin ti some 500 page in aa, as weel as the completion seen o 'An In-Memoriam', as weel as some prose memoirs o RAF time, essays an meditations on this an thon.

'An In-Memoriam' will aye mynd me o the day ma faither taen the turn at killt him finally, for he haundit me the diskette o it for prentin oot aerlier that same Saturday. It daels wi an hauds the feck o aa the poems he iver made anent members o the Law faimlie, an it wis collectit thegither for thaim. Here an thare it uises some o the same poems at kythes in 'Yeegie Landscapes'. He didna intend it for publication, as he intendit monie ither o his poem-getherins ti be published, but it haes been sae waarmlie spoken aboot bi some o its readers at mibbie it'll see licht o day some time.

T S Law

Scadda

The scadda o the past owerhaills oor praisent,
an unco weerd o that groo clood growein daurker
wi ilka day that gloams mair lyker mortclaith.
It owerhaills baith the waiker an the sterker,
an thaem the certain-shair that thocht them siccar
at onie tyme and intae onie place
lik muckle trees they thocht tae see growe bigger
an be thursels the bigger in that growein.

Lik the lave, they nae mair kent thur wy o growthe
nor bairns can ken thur licht is on the blink
that cannae see the glim that maks thur youth
lowp on afore they ken thursels perjink
and intae eild that slavers at the mooth.

We aa gang doonwart till we're lyke tae sink
intae the yird lik auld howffs, that's the truith.
Lik deein treees, oor days the bous sair bent,
ligg orrie on the gress, oor tyme fair spent
wi the auntrin twigs twychilderlyke for pruif
we did oor devoirs, sat in schuil, tuk tent
as guid bairns dae, or sae we yaist tae think.

We are the gress amang the brakkent bous.
We tap the winnock-soles o thae auld howffs
we made oorsels o, till in lang, lang days
we mak the gress that maks them yince again
the brawest hooses man's and habitable.

But lang, lang syne afore, we focht a battle
wi thae doore maisters o oor hamelie yirth,
thae sentinels, the nettles o the hirth.

Lik a banner abuin the heech o the brae, monie the yin
bears the gree fae Tyme an clooters that Auld Yin doorelie
i the bygaun or he bous the lyart heid. A wheen o us,
the gy twychildert i the haerns, crawl thru the stoor
langhamein lyke the cloke yince aiblins the paer auld grannie.
We spit oor daith for that bit bodie's oor
i the hinmaist nicht whoe can weel dae nocht mair
nor wheenge an wheechle or the scythe is sherpent
for thon fell strak that faas on rich an paer,
and ever did we mynd whoe stuid or ran.

Nae hirplin sklim for me abuin thon brae!
Gie me the virr tae breenge, syne nicht ma day!

Hungers

S'she, "Are ye pie-hungerie or are
ye paistrie-hungerie?" The pie is verie,
but paistrie's mair a dentie kinna preeve,
no juist lik whiskie-hunger: that 's the rarest
o the hungers. But grund-hunger, gin ye please,
can whyles gar fermers phantisise on ease
has nocht avaa adae, as ye may guess,
wi yon yird-hunger o the fey that gies
mools hunger-hunger's gutsiness.

The Hero

Gin Cuchulain had never been, nor thon lustre o his days,
the heroics o his devoirs bleezin fae his broo lik the rays
o the ayebydein staur caad Ireland, thare'd never hae been
the sang tae sing it, nor the singer tae inspire
the lieges even-on thru years as green
wi hope as the machair wi the rain, or as ruid wi the fire
o anger as the sea wi the wastren sun can show it:
it's a paer bit growthe that has nae grund alow it.

Lae thaem alane, the folk, juist let them byde
lik the gress for the feck o three thoosan year an mair,
whyles growein lik a steerin laddie, whyles ill-guydit,
a lad o pairts but the pairts gy ill-divydit,
but aye abuin aathing, thursel, that nocht can hyde,
no even the desolatioun o despair.

Table Bay

My thoughts are like the winds that race
across the gray-green ocean face.
    The winds waves lace in Table Bay.
    It's fare-ye-well and fair away.

Like the blue-crystal-breaking sea,
your image alters quietly.
    And I must leave this Table Bay.
    It's fare-ye-well and fair away.

Now like the seagull's swaying flight
you glance and dip before my sight.
    The white light shines on Table Bay.
    It's fare-ye-well and fair away.

Stay you my heart and stay my need.
The long, low, browning hills recede.
    The seaways lead to Table Bay.
    It's fare-ye-well and fair away.

Tay Pearl

Whaa reads as easilie as this is written
kens nocht is skeelie that's laid past less care.
Yit lay this bye ye till yer guid doon-sittin
can gar it growe groo licht as onie pearl
intae the Tay an bonnie, caller, rare.
Here is yer mairriage wi yersel and hame
as tho yer benner sheen were bebblin cleir
as grace laid bye ye till it lichts the same
    lang gaet lays past yer fame.

T S Law til Margaret Rose Law on our Golden Wedding day 22/3/1997

Mixter-Maxterie

To blessed and long memory
that has been ben folk like myself
who like to tell the wee bit story
about the where that they had gone,
and pleasure in the place they found;
and those among my family names
as well, who told where they had been,
remembering that place of pleasure
in Ireland where the lovely airt
was Ulster, not to be forgotten.

And to long, blessed memory
of people like myself, who once
were in the wee bit story telling
about the whereabouts they stayed
when they had found a pleasant place,
as did the other family names
who went where they would speak about
their pleasure in a place remembered
in Scotland, airted bonnilie:
like Ulster, not to be forgotten.

But I would ask them all to mind
the Irish foot upon Dunadd
first brought the Irish here to Scotland
around the time an Anglic foot
first climbed a hill and called it law;
for those were like the hottering
of oatmeal in a porridge pot,
who melled, fleeing the Dunadd midges
to be the kind of folk like me
whiles airted Ireland, airted Scotland.

The Sodger
Fae the Afrikaans o Uys Krige

In siccan a dreech ootlin orrie airt
ane wurld an groo but growthieness
that skyles in aa its sairie stanes
or the groo gangs lirt i the luft
sae nane may lippen ont,
his leefou lane
alang the stoorie pad
traiks
the lane sodger lad.

Abuin is the furst nicht staur,
abuin Fort Wajier liggin awo sae faur.

Alanerlie
the lane sodger lad
his leefou lane.
His leefou lane
wi a wurld o dool an luve
yirdit apairt
in the howff o his ain hert
that nane save he can prove.

His leefou lane
dreechlie in the desert dayligaun
that sweels aroond him lik the groo scaum
o the sperflin stoor
as the haevie ammo buits plowter the saund attoore.

An Fort Wajier
– oasis alane in this haill wilderness
whaur ilka bink an rowe o the camel pad maun gang,
whaur nuintyde murls amang the leafs in the sooch o a saft wuin,
whaur aathing cawed tae the hunkers wi heat funds beild tae byde
ane airt alanerlie whaur the palms skinkle siller i the muin, an
whaur deep, deep, doon aneath the stye black waas, the whyte
waal watters hain in;
anerlie the yin snode airt
whaur leerielicht, guid watter an scran, an the crack o men
pleesure the hert –
aneath the furst nicht staur
liggin awo sae faur.

Wi his helmet on his heid,
bandolier roond his breist,
watter-bottle on his hip,
rifle ower his shoother,

he traiks amang the stoor:
a groo-graithit taet
againss the mair groo
o the ondeemas luft
o the doore orrie erd

in sicna groo border
whaur the nicht
mells a weird wi the bricht
as the licht aye maun sperfle
amang the groo scadda.

Abuin is the furst nicht staur,
abuin Fort Wajier liggin awo sae faur.

A groo-graithit taet
gainss groo-graithit creatioun.
An the sodger traiks on,
traiks on
aye traiks on
alang the stoorie desert pad,
and his scadda raxin slawlie an siccarlie,
cawed attoore the groo pad
ower a binsh o broon lavastane,
intil the thorn buss.

The sodger's scadda
faas ower the desert.

The sodger's scadda
faas ower Africa.

Stievelik an sterklik an black wi aa dreedour,
ower the haill wurld
faas the sodger's black scadda.

Abuin is the furst nicht staur,
abuin Fort Wajier liggin awo sae faur.

The Curse an the Blessin

For thaem that ancientlie kept Colonsay
an kept the laws o the Lordes o the Isles i thur day,
hae peetie, Scotland, ower yer braid demesne:
see, black as the yirth cuid faa on Oran's ee
whan Chattan Sanct was Oran's brither nane,
the auld sair curse still yokes on Clan MacPhie.
Here 's dool! Thir folk that had the haill sea at thur wish
cannae hae the yae bit saumon for a fish.

Tho the best o makars wuidnae steer his shanks
for less nor a lass, nor a singin fiere, nor a dram,
(for aa thegither, man, he 'd lowp the muin)
yit makars aye were tinkler-lyke: this yin,
for MacPhie an freedom, gies his rhymin thanks,
tho Scotland daesnae gie a tinkler's damm.

Excerpt frae *Yeegie Landscapes*

"There's naething," said the Union leader,
"lik a wee bit hate tae steer them up!"
And then there was another Wullie
street-cornering in Newarthill
one miserable night as chilly
as cold rain blirting through snell wind
that fuffed about the gable-end
of public house where not one maik
could jingle with another stiver
among the menfolk there to pay
for even the single warming half
would make a body tolerant.

Poor menfolk there, dispiritedly
crowded against the gable-end,
the worse for those edged into rainfall,
hands into empty pockets sunk,
and hunched-up shoulders shielding faces,
as in among them, muttering
dejected as the drizzle, stilled
despairingly to dowie silence.

Out of the onding of the raining,
a biscuit van came trundling by
and slooshed them from the sloonjing highway,
as momentarily lamplight
picked out upon the passing lorry
this legend on heraldic arms,
*By Appointment to His Majesty
the King*, like ancient battle-standard.

Among the men the rain among
there was a deeper silence stilling
itself into a silence deep
and deeper still than probes forever
the silence of the mind in making
the tongue silence articulate
with sound made manifestly senseful.

Then Wullie stepped out of the shelter
was comfort of the gable-end,
his shoulders hunched against the bluffert,
face snarling at the wheeching van
that disappeared along the road
among the dark gray sheen of rain:
"Ay, thare gaes he," he sniftered coldly,
"And I'm gy shair the bluidie Keeng
haes neever etten a single yin
o MacVeetie an Price's buggerin bakes!"

Veesit

This morn, as gyan dreech as eer was seen,
the luft "as black as the Earl o Hell's waistcoat",
(speaking clicheticallie as auld-farrant)
 wi the auntrin stoond o thunner yonnerwys,
yit here I wauken chirpie as a lintie,
 myndin George Todd is comein here fae Spain,
and as it happens, juist as I'm re-readin
yon screed, *Garcia Lorca* bi Edwin Honig.

I tell a lee: tae tell the truith, I luk
aboot me lyke an ee upon the mornin
no blearie, but as waukrif as oot-keekin
 upon a luft no black, but wi a haur
as groo as gars gruein come up the backbaen
 lik wunnerin whoere suimmertyme haes gane
sin thon timm beddin doon as croose as cosie
tae speir for dreamin naething lyke a nichtmeir.

Och but, the waather's whit we mak oorsels,
for am I no masel as chirpie-cheerie
as fair in tid wi whit's athin the mornin,
 nae maitter groolie daurk, or blue abuin
lik een o bairnies inwrocht roond as bonnie:
 I ken fyne I am in guid tid, because
here an I intil makkin twoe-three verses
tae waalcome in the mornin, singin o it.

I ken the waather's aften guid in Spain,
but Spain is no the whit we 'll be colloguin:
maist lykelie it will be oorsels we 'll speak o,
 for aa the wurld is naething but oorsels
the onie tyme the onie chiel is neebor
 lik chowe the auntrin shaef or pree the scone,
sae here 's tae whit 's tae come, as tho the gannin
were faur awo the yit an no the morra.

A Short Memory of Dale

Iain Bahlaj

I first met Dale at the child psychiatrist. I had been going for three weeks. I usually spoke to the psychiatrist about ambitions and goals. I wrote ten down but, at the time, I never wanted to achieve them.

"Sometimes it's good to have no feeling."

He sat next to me and introduced himself as Dale. His name consisted only of initials. His full title, he told me, was Dale Andrew Laurence Edward Scott. They were the names of his four great-grandfathers. Three of whom died in wars. He didn't say which wars.

"But that's no big deal," he told me.

We sat and looked at the posters on the clipboard. I read the number for Childline out loud, and he whistled an old song. One my gran knows. I asked him what was wrong. Why he was there.

"I have a condition," he told me, smiling. "My legs sometimes go weak. I can't feel anything."

"Really?" I said, "that's a shame."

"Sometimes it's good to have no feeling."

We sat in silence then the psychiatrist appeared. He asked me to follow him and he asked Dale why he was early.

"I like it here," Dale told him.

I walked into the room and stared at the colour chart on the wall, listing people's reactions to situations, including "mum asks me to tidy room" and "teacher tells me to stop talking . . ." I sat in a soft orange chair and the psychiatrist fondled his long, black hair, then took a pen from the pocket of his tight striped shirt.

We looked at my list. He asked me questions about the cutting. I told him it had gone. I told him all the razor blades in the house had been removed.

"Do you still want to do it?"

"I don't know," I said.

"Do you cry sometimes, I mean, lately?"

"No."

We spoke about music and I mentioned an old band and he told me his favourite band and I felt embarrassed for him.

The session went past and I went home. The psychiatrist told me "until next week."

Dale waved and rose from his chair. I noticed the backs of his knees. When he exerted pressure on the knee joints they twitched and threatened to give way. The weather was cold. It was dry.

Two weeks of nothing passed. I watched someone vomit into a brown bag at school, then choke. Their face turned red. It was a girl. Her face turned purple. My German teacher approached me and complimented me on my understanding of the language, and I told her I spoke fluently when I lived in Dusseldorf. I sat and watched the posters, which included posters highlighting the issues of domestic abuse, sexual abuse, drug abuse, alcohol abuse. The sexual abuse poster featured a girl sitting in a corner, curled into a ball, her hands clasped over her knees.

"They're all like that," I said to Dale when he stumbled into the waiting room.

"What are?"

"The child abuse posters, they're all like that."

He looked at the poster and said yes quietly.

We sat in silence. A fat girl with ginger hair and visible scars on her wrists walked by. A thin, bony girl with sunken eyes stood by the telephone, flicking through a telephone book. The weight of the book appeared to strain her arms. She breathed heavily and I watched her eyelids slowly descend, before a bell ringing jolted her.

"I had a dream last night," Dale said. "I was walking down a corridor, looking at strange paintings on the walls. I met a boy and girl, and they looked healthy. Then their skin started to slowly pale, then turn blue. They both took razor blades and started to cut their arms. I sat and watched. I wanted to ask them to cut their faces off. Finally, I did."

I asked him what happened.

"They cut their faces off," he said.

He turned and grinned. His smile looked lazy, his eyes seemed tired. I laughed at his dream. He asked me if I ever felt the urge to bleed a little bit.

"Yeah, sometimes."

"Can I see?"

I pulled up the sleeves of my jersey. He looked at my scars and smiled gently. I showed him the scar which was infected. The scar which ran from my forearm to my shoulder.

I rolled up my jeans and showed him the scars on my legs.

"What about you?" I said.

He grinned and rolled up his trouser leg. A scar, shaped like an eye, dominated his skin just above the knee. His shin was opened in several places. "I've seen the bone," he told me. "It's not hard to reach it."

"Didn't it hurt too bad?" I said. "I usually cut the usual areas. I cut my legs but only the fronts, from my knees to my body. I don't cut the backs, or the shins."

"I cut the backs, too," he said.

He twisted his leg, using his hands. One hand jerked and seemed to die. The backs of his legs were covered in deep scars, all shaped like eyes, red and fiery. "I'm not letting God do all the work," he told me, grinning. "My legs don't work, cutting them makes no difference."

"Right."

We sat in silence. The psychiatrist came and asked me to follow him.

We talked about goals and ambitions. I told him a goal would be to go to a football match. I didn't want to. He asked me which team I supported.

When I passed Dale on the way out he rose from his seat and his legs collapsed beneath him. He shook and fell, landing on the polished floor.

The receptionist ran to help him up. He smiled and started to laugh.

Two weeks of nothing passed. Two people, father and son, died. The father died from cancer and the son had a heart attack. The son suffered from obesity and they had to take his body out on a reinforced stretcher. It took six men to lift it. The wife and mother, a woman called Mary, sat and watched, hypnotised, as one of the men dropped his end of the stretcher, causing the body to fall, and bump against the concrete. I watched from my room.

Renate, the German assistant, asked me where I had lived in Germany and I told her I lived in Bonn and found the city beautiful and engaging.

I sat and read graffiti printed on the wall of the waiting room. Laura is a fat bitch. Ross is a faggot and sucks cocks. I thought herpes was a shampoo until I caught it. Easter rising. Fuck the pope.

An old woman walked around in circles, mumbling something under her breath. The receptionist approached her and held her arm gently. The receptionist told the old woman that she was not in hospital, that the hospital was down the street, on the left.

The woman screamed and fell. She lay on the floor, motionless. Her eyes remained open and she looked at me. The receptionist lifted her up and slowly pulled her to a seat. "This happens all the time, Marge," she said.

I tapped on my seat. The old woman looked at me and the room was filled with the smell of urine. A nurse appeared and took the old woman away. The seat was wet.

My psychiatrist came and asked me to follow him. I told him that things were going well. I said that the suicide attempt was a one-off. "I'll never do it again," I told him. We spoke about music and he started singing a heavy metal song. We both got embarrassed. He stopped and I asked him how much he was paid.

He wouldn't tell me and we sat in silence.

"Have you any idea why Dale isn't here?" he asked after a few minutes.

"No."

"Oh," he said, looking bored. "Dale had an accident and he's dead. He cut the main artery at the back of his leg, and bled to death. He actually *pulled* the artery from his leg before cutting it. He also cuts tendons, ligament, and muscle tissue. Does that *bother* you?"

He looked angry. I sat and considered the question. I felt tired.

"*Does that affect you in any way?*" he said, his voice rising in volume.

"No," I replied. I exhaled deeply and scanned the walls for any new posters. A drawing of a heart hung on a clipboard, with a message saying "we miss you, Dale" and a poor drawing of an angel, which looked more like Tinkerbell.

"*Well,*" the psychiatrist said. "I think that is about it, you don't need to see me any more, I think you're fine."

"Okay."

I stood up and walked slowly out, saying goodbye politely on the way. I passed a crying girl in the corridor. Her eye shadow covered her cheeks.

Jane Austen, Socialist Soccerbabe

David McVey

Much of my career, and a fair proportion of my academic reputation, I have given over to refuting cheap criticisms of Jane Austen, Queen of the English novel. Only an insensitive, ill-read savage could accuse Austen's work of being exclusive, closeted and lacking in context. So what if Austen never mentions the Napoleonic Wars? Irvine Welsh has not, so far, attempted an in-depth historical analysis of Trafalgar. There are no disquistions on the battle of Austerlitz in the novels of Will Self or Martin Amis. Why pick on Austen just because she happened to live during the period? She may have had strong reasons to forget the wars: and perhaps she had other abiding passions that put the follies of nations in proper perspective. I would advance her recently rediscovered unfinished novel, *On Me 'Ead, Son!* which she intended to publish under the pseudonym 'Nosher' Austen. The following extract is from the first chapter.

> On the third morning of his stay at Bath, Mr Heartsby took the waters, using the opportunity to consider the import of his interview with Emily. It had been grossly injurious to his feelings that the young lady who had taken residence in his heart should have cried so insistently, "Football! Football! That is all you ever think about, Mr Heartsby!"
>
> As he was conveyed to the Assembly Rooms in his commodious carriage, he came to a decision. He cried to the coachman to stop and bade him procure a runner. When such a youth was produced, Mr Heartsby handed him a hastily-scribbled note. "Take that to Sir Richard Ormthwaite, and there'll be a florin for you!" The youth ran off with celerity.
>
> Soon, in the rooms he had taken for the season, Sir Richard was unfolding the newly delivered note.
>
> "Ah!" he exclaimed to Lady Agatha, who was taking a turn about the room, "I do believe tis from young Heartsby. Egad ! He wishes to be considered for Saturday's match against Meryton Athletic ! How refreshing that a man with five thousand a year should still wish to chase the round ball in pursuit of the noble game! I can, then, dispense with the services of the Scandinavian trialist." Lady Agatha tut-tutted and merely remarked that it was unduly warm for the time of year. Then, with an imperious flourish of her skirts, she swept out of the room, leaving Sir Richard to ponder the reshaping of his back four.

There are those who do not welcome this broadening of Austen's subject matter. Fans of both *Fever Pitch* and *The Thistle and the Grail* must now admit that the football novel had an earlier, greater Genesis.

In recent years, several feminist writers have torn *Pride and Prejudice* to shreds trying to find traces of sisterhood-friendly protest. They have portrayed Austen's mild satire about the subjection of middle-class womanhood as a kind of rampant suffragism. They are clutching at straws. Austen's attack on the social order in her best-known novel is much more direct. Few, however, are aware of the alternative ending to *Pride and Prejudice,* where characters that have appeared only fleetingly, or who have lurked unseen in the background, crowd centre stage. The Bennets' servants and their families, coachmen and agricultural labourers converge in one pitchfork-waving crowd, and confront the gentry, including the Bennets.

The leader of the mob, a low, ill-dressed fellow, who had formerly been in service at Longbourn, motioned for the crowd to be quiet. He then turned and addressed the ladies and gentlemen.

"The house and grounds of Longbourn be now under the control of the Meryton Workers' Soviet. For too long you fine folks have expropriated the surplus value of our labour. . ."

"This is a most unfortunate thing you and your accomplices have done, Ned Lowton," interjected a gentleman, "Methinks you will soon pay with your head!"

"We have nothing to lose but our chains, Sir Robert! This be just the first spark in a fiery revolution that will sear all England and beyond with its flame! Then where be your fine carriages and your expensive clothes and your grand balls at Netherfield Hall?" Briefly, Lowton's eyes fell on Mr Bennet. He lowered his voice a little as he addressed only his former employer. "I ain't got no personal argument with you, Mr Bennet. I don't deny you was a reasonable master by your own lights. But the weaknesses of the capitalist economy are structural and their solution must not be mitigated by personal concerns. All masters are to be interned. It be a matter of personal regret to me that you will be separated from Mrs Bennet."

"On the contrary, Lowton, I feel you do me a great favour."

"Well, men," said Lowton, again addressing his followers, "Let the collectivisation of local agriculture begin! Workers of the World, unite!" A loud, raucous hurrah was raised. Mrs Bennet condemned the whole business as most upsetting to her nerves and demanded to be allowed to return home. For her interjection she was prodded with a pitchfork.

The decision to employ the conventional, happy-ever-after ending, in which everyone gets married and ends up smiling benignly at everyone else, must surely have been forced on Austen by a terrified publisher. As a result of this corporate timidity, Austen is denied the reputation she deserves as a searching, challenging, radical artist. Some have questioned, or even ridiculed, the authenticity of the manuscripts from which these excerpts have been taken. The criticisms do not trouble me: I will explain how I traced the originals and offer conclusive evidence of their origins in my forthcoming literary biography *Jane Austen in Yer Face!* However, I do intend, here, to answer some of the more frequent, ill-advised criticisms.

The internal evidence of the manuscripts, many critics have said, points to much later work by a much later writer. Some have even hinted that *I* am the author. Specifically, they have pointed to the frequent use in *On Me 'Ead, Son!* of phrases and terms which seem more appropriate to a more recent period. How could Austen have used and mastered the terminology of association football when the invention of the game was still some time away? Similarly, in the alternative ending to *Pride and Prejudice*, the manuscript suggests a form of Marxist Communism that was more than half-a-century in the future. Indeed, the excerpt I have included here appears to borrow some of its phasing from *Capital* and *The Communist Manifesto*.

The makers of these criticisms do not understand the nature of literary genius. The giants of creative literature do not inhabit the same constrict-

82

ing, present-haunted world as the rest of us. Instead, their imaginations range freely back and forth through the ages, returning only to the prison of the present when they choose to do so. Scientists will never crack the problem of time travel: creative writers already have. That Austen should grasp ideas and realities from the future she would never live to see, surprises no-one who comprehends the magnitude of her talent.

The apparent plagiarism from Marx is easily explained. Marx himself was aware of Austen's writing. He may have had access to the lesser known works and unpublished manuscripts at the British Museum Library. So, no Austen-aping charlatan (neither me nor anyone else) echoed Marx's words: the truth is that *Marx borrowed from Austen!* Some of the most ringing phrases in the Socialist canon originated not with Karl Marx, but with the supposedly sheltered clergyman's daughter from Bath.

Those who do not accuse me of literary fraud suggest instead that I am credulous and deluded. Equally untrue: I have gone out of my way to denounce extreme theories about Austen's writing. For example, I reject as a fake the alternative version of *Emma* (entitled *Elvis*) which some writers claim demonstrates that Austen was the true inventor of rock 'n' roll.

To present Jane Austen for the post-modern age, it isn't necessary to suggest that she wrote the lyrics to *My Baby Left Me*. I believe my case to be radical enough: Jane Austen was the original beat writer. She was the first soccerchick and remains the true Queen of cool, the ultimate radical babe of the English novel!

Angus Calder

Dipa's Bowl
for Kaiser Haq, January 1999

A gift ten years old, Dipa's bowl
has sat on my best bookcase
beside postcards of Kali
and texts by Finlay,
under the long nose and hooded eyes
of my statuette of Ogun
a painter's imagination
of Sappho, mother of all,
and a photograph of MacNeice
my particular master.

When I've spoken of this assemblage
as my personal shrine,
I have not been joking.

Now I pick up her gift, varnished
papier mache (I think) patterned
white on blue, in an eastwest mode
between Picasso and purdah's
culture where God has no face
but abstract motifs insist on
art's immanence everywhere.

Triangles, squares, button roundels
brim over its elegance.
Under my 100-watt bulb
it glows with moonlight.
Where I picked it up,
dusting it with my thumb
there is discreet red stippling and
now I see that a casual-seeming
dash of muted blood red (as if
from a cut finger, hers, a fixing of her
lifejuice, swift intention or lucky mistake)
was the point of Dipa's pattern.

Blood on the moon; an image
from Lorca's Granada, but this
light I conceive is denser yet
lighter, more fragile light,
as when cool dawn will soon creep in
over a huge river.

This bowl is as light as whatever
soul we could possibly have
might be while still outweighing
your pale fax through my machine
seven a.m., cold Sunday,
to tell me of a death
which algebraically
I perhaps can credit
no more if no less than you do,
except that for you loss must weigh
like compacted darkness, while I
just now handle persisting lightness
and remember light.

Zentime in Caithness

Figured in clouds black against pear-pale sunset,
a demented giant baglady
rushes to Orkney, chased hard
by Hephaistos puffing at his furnace,
slavering dugs, and a furious crocodile.
Yet earlier, as if wafted by these
intransigencies looming up behind them,
cloudlets had passed so graciously
over iron-grey sea turning navy blue,
as if yesterday's rainbow was indeed a promise
blessing whatever seafarers pursue,
sweet little sixteen, and the evergreen islands
such as Caithness itself might have seemed,
when Norsemen saw
fertility, the chance of peace,
sixteen, twenty-five, forty, more
good times of faithful barley returning.

The Fourth Craw

Darling, you know
such peculiar cold of loneliness
better than I do – that chilly space
of the individual bird, flockless, which flies
with its dinosaur destiny
to skeletal future –
but can't somehow we share it,
two flitters, always in quest
of the fourth craw
who wisnae there at a'?

On the Inverness Train
For David Morrison

"Flat with bumps" –
from the train, as you promised, I witness
this big-sky country, brightlit misty Caithness
where lochans and little oxbows
glitter by dark plantations
under cumulus, and the whitewash of farmtouns
is midgetted by the vast angelic
illumination of the longest clouds.
But now, over there, a riposte, peatlight,
such warm brownness confronting that blue
and being something different. Oh, barley,
barley – we chug on
into a territory of wasted dances
and frail last leaves on birches, mischancy
Sutherland – however, suddenly,
somewhere, a grove
by a salmon river in delightful November
weather, Kildonan, yes, smirr, yes,
but then a rainbow past Kildonan.

Haymarket Sunset
for Sandy Robb

That lass in a woolly cap with earflaps
waiting at dusk for a bus by Haymarket Station
may conceivably have mince for brains
but at least her delicate profile and clear eyes
suggest potential. The young have not yet
been defeated, their gaze is towards tomorrow,
their step is forward. I stare back over decades –
so many times at this busstop as sunset,
salmon and jade, has ebbed behind Corstorphine.
As I ride out once again to curling, my
tomorrows are fewer – however, week by week,
even hour by hour, Murrayfield ice is always
different. You have to adjust your weight,
your line, your sweep. And this light is always beautiful.

Chilly Summer in Ross

One

This wind blusters down Loch Broom
as if it ettles
to headbutt what's left of summer
or like a white ball aimed to scatter
would-be-ruddy apples and the green
baubles on the chestnut trees –
but summer stands:
hills balk the wind grimly.
Wind will be copped and handcuffed,
snookered, as calm
returns and the grey bay settles.

Two

Here in the hilly north, for no clear reason,
I remember premature, quirky dead ones
– Geoff, fellow student who flung himself under a tube train
– Jim, first met with Bandaid across his spec lens
who carcrashed in Lesotho
– Phil, who fell off a mountain
and Allan who fell down some steps in a New Town lane.
Surely any air anywhere should tingle with menace?
Not here, just now. The grey sky is massively calm.
Wagtails flit. There is little traffic
and in light like milk
quiet houses stand clean-whitewashed.
Yet I must remember, without panic
that here, too, disaster has its fishing season.

Address by the Bardies to Edwin Morgan on his Eightieth

To think you've reached the big eight-o, still
dancing on a high trapeze with your demon
above the implacable void! Even if we get there,
we'll never catch you up. The sorry semen
which spawned us lacked your genes. It's no fair.
Yet, fired by the example of your will
to taste all words, let not one go unsavoured,
we'll mebbe craft a poem or two between us
to prove how much, by you, we have been favoured.
Pending such, our last frail rhyme, of course, is 'genius'.

Miss-myth
written with Douglas, aged 10

When the Reindeer People
confronted Santa Claus
they were most upset.
He went about their wigwams shouting,
"I want a reindeer with a red nose!!!"
They retorted, "We won't give you a reindeer
but we'll give you a red nose
with our special glowing spray paint,
offer ends December 25."
But, Santa said, pathetically,
"All I want is a burly reindeer
to drive my difficult sleigh."
Reindeer Shaman replied,
"We would love to rev you up, sir, but . . ."

At this point Evil Hedgehog remarked,
"Notice our handsome barbecue spit.
Please step indoors, we will dress you up for it, sir.
You will be a most welcome kebab."
Inside poor old Santa
at last met Moominmamma.
She said, "If you will consent to be an icecube,
you can be frozen for a billion years.
Then Hello Doom Speaking
will tell you that global warming
has burnt the world to cinders.

Bad luck, Santa, you just can't win."
Heads I win, tails you lose . . .
so he sizzled fine
on Hedgehog's spit.

Colin Dunbar

When creating a new piece my main concerns are to focus on the psychological aspects of the sitter and to breathe life into them. I love the challenge of creating a solid 3D figure existing within its own space in a two-dimensional medium. This started in my youth when I painted murals on every wall in my bedroom of characters culled from films, comics, photographs and my imagination. I tried to make them as realistic as possible and I still do though my painting style has grown and matured.

When working on print-making and drawings, I'm most conscious of trying to suggest atmosphere with streaky swirls of etching ink and creating beautiful lines with the pencil or etching needle. These images are mostly influenced by contemporary graphic novels though I am interested in the etchings of many great artists. This year has been busy. I have been steadily commissioned to paint portraits and am planning an exhibition in Edinburgh with two artists, Simon Kidd and Daniel Plant.

I was staying at George Bruce's house through the winter in 1998 and was commissioned by his family to paint his portrait for his 90th birthday. George himself had commissioned me to create a portrait for his friend and editor, Lucina, and this project prompted the discovery of a wish to paint on a larger scale than previously. I produced many sketches and an etching before starting to paint the portraits, the first of which attempted to capture the intelligence and concentration of a creative mind. George is depicted at a slightly off-kilter angle with eyes closed and his head surrounded by a calm blue and white background.

For the second painting I produced rough sketches, one depicting George standing with the North Sea in the background and this seemed easily the most fitting of all the various studies. The sea, and those who rely on it for a living, is a topic that George often discusses. The sea also seems the perfect metaphor for conveying the drama and movement that surround George, as can be seen in his new book *Pursuit*.

I soon realised that if the background was a moving mass of water then it would work in the painting's favour if the sitter was animated also. George's portrait is landscape-shaped, which meant that only head and shoulders would be visible. In the painting, George is reciting (as he often did while he sat for me) and the movement is achieved by animating his face with lively brushstrokes, particularly the mouth and eyes. I have been interested in people's thoughts and reactions to this portrait and am delighted that its new home is in the Scottish National Portrait Gallery.

Editor's note:

This feature of the work of artist Colin Dunbar, portraitist of George Bruce, is the first of what will become a regular feature of *Chapman*. It is also part of a larger agenda to develop the magazine in range, style, design and content, and to extend its reach across artistic genres.

Self-portrait, graphite on paper

'She saw a young man', monoprint etching
drawn from short story by American writer Peter Straub

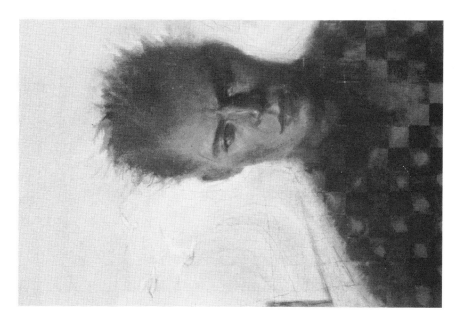

'Alien', monoprint etching
'Landing Point: Earth Beach', oil on board

Portrait of Magnus Linklater, oil on canvas

'Karen', monoprint etching

'St Staine's Night', monoprint etching
drawn from a poem by Peter Redgrove,

Reviews

A New Day Dawning

A New Day Dawning: A Portrait of Ireland in 1900, Daniel Mulhall, The Collins Press, £19.99. *Banríon Álainn an Lionáin,* Trans: Micheál Ó Conghaile, £6.00; *Sna Fir,* Micheál Ó Conghaile, £10.00; *Fís Angus Teanga,* Eds: Padraic Reaney and Micheál Ó Conghaile, £6.00; *An Phlluais Ama,* Claire Dagger, £4.00: all Clo Iar Chonnachta.

The arrival of Daniel Mulhall in summer 1998 as the first Irish Consul General to Scotland has led to some memorable, liquid-fuelled, cultural collaborations and celebrations. His initial St Patrick's Day party was just controlled mayhem. Just. Further on, Bloomsday (June 16th), led to the wonderful sight of Joyce McMillan sighing out the sex-laden cadences of Molly in the new Consulate building in Randolph Crescent. A visit, with this reviewer, to the Oxford Bar ended with the manager John Gates presenting Mulhall with the pub tie (a cow astride a gate is the motif) and an invite to play with the pub's five-aside football team. In literary terms his initial foray was to write an elegant introduction for the Irish issue of *Chapman* (No 92). Now this Waterford born diplomat, who qualified as a historian, has turned author.

His debut with *A New Day Dawning* is a delight. Lucidly written, it is a literary/ photographic recreation of Ireland a century ago. Another deeply satisfying dimension is its designated sense of purpose to represent peace imperatives in Ireland and a dedicated projection for the initiatives that Mulhall and his fellow would-be peace-makers installed in the 'Good Friday Agreement' of 1998. His diplomatic appointment is part of the parcel of that 'commune' of the Isles.

This allows, explores and expresses the palpable fact that there is more depth to 'New Ireland' than a British newspaper slogan. Even if the phrase of today's tabloids, 'The Celtic Tiger', owes more to the Esso petrol logo than the words of William Blake. Mulhall elevates literature, and particularly poetry, to a central position in new Irish thinking. Yeats's indignation gives way to Heaney's informed questioning. There is confidence in the therapy.

As the book opens, we are in Ireland on the eve of the 20th century: 1900. Scotland have beaten Ireland 9-1 in Glasgow. In Dublin Yeats has returned from London to help organise a National Theatre. A failed musician is just back from the Gaelic speaking Aran Islands where he has conceived the glimmer of an idea for a play. *Fool in the Family* is his working title. Fortunately by 1907 it will have become *The Playboy of the Western World.* Angst personified prowls the urban streets and is called James Joyce. Also on the streets are mobs and monarchists. In South Africa the Boer War has attracted a fighting brigade of Irish nationalists led by Major John McBride. He is later to marry Maude Gonne, the love of Yeats's life. Eventually he is executed in 1916. In 1900 Queen Victoria is not amused. She pays her third and final visit to the 'Emerald Isle' colony. The workhouse destitutes are kicked out and told to wave flags at her. Maude Gonne in retaliation empties the schools and tells the kids to wave fists.

Mulhall then moves out of the capital. Bleakly he records the contemporary emigration figures. If those of the Famine years were heart-breaking the new figures are not much better. There is a loss of 5 million people in the previous decade. The world's largest per capita Temperance Society is organised throughout Ireland. Alcohol reigns. The Irish experience is deftly related to British and other European trends. A deep, if quiet, indignation underlies these statistical accounts.

In South Dublin Sir Horace Plunkett MP, representative of the Irish Unionist Party, is forming the Co-operative Movement. This will for many decades mould the lucrative Dairy Industry. His own home is later torched by patriots. Also in Dublin the polemic and prolific journalist David Patrick Moran uses *The Leader* to propose the unthinkable. A land led and ruled by the Irish. Later he turns bigot and his rabid nationalism leads to him being pilloried by Joyce in *Ulysses*. In Belfast sitting Unionist T W Russell propagates an all-island unity and optimism. He is vilified as a traitor by his fellow citizens and their fearful cohorts. These vignettes are recorded not as revisionist apologies but as reportage on disputes, divides and consequences.

In his final chapters Mulhall addresses contemporary themes and mores. He questions the emphasis of many received perceptions. The perspective of hindsight becomes tenuous. Those founders of 20th century Irish martyrdom and materialism, Patrick Pearse and De Valera, are therapeutically analysed:

Give them their just place as historical figures no longer encumbered by an association with contemporary atrocities.

This is strange and somewhat wonderful from a champion of Fianna Fail.

He assesses that Ireland 'Now' began in 1973 with European membership rather than the struggles of 1916 or the bitter infighting of 1921. This is a clear-sighted analysis of the virtue of assimilation rather than the dishonouring of an honourable historical past.

This handsome production from a Cork imprint is wonderfully illustrated by postcards and photographs. It is an apt and recommended account of how an attributable past can positively refuel attitudes for the future.

A visit this year to Ireland coincided with the stage premiere of Micheál Ó Conghaile's Gaelic (Irish) translation of Martin McDonagh's award-winning play *The Beauty Queen of Leenane*. Direct by Diarmuid de Faoite in the Samuel Beckett Centre in Trinity College Dublin it was a night of interpretations of old roles and a vivid renewal with my first language. The play in English, even when first performed by Druid Theatre Company in 1996, underwhelmed me. I came to it late so maybe I was influenced by the over-emphatic praise and the patronising sound of British critics applauding 'another' new Irish writer.

The four characters are hymned by a narrator who talks of rural aesthetics; personal, domestic and emotional. Generation gaps guide to specific judgements becoming universal opinions. Set in Connemara, the conclusion seems to be that the West is awake and about to hum a new song. Ó Conghaile's translation gives words to the tune, lyricism to the language. The play has plot, becoming, as real theatre must, a treacherous minefield.

This ability and willingness to interpret new themes in an emerging Gaelteacht gives a liberating force to Ó Conghaile's first novel *Sna Fir*. At times I found language too dense for relaxed reading but re-reading is rewarding. It tells of a Gay Gaelic-speaking Everyman searching not so much for happiness as content in the strange land that is Ireland Now. The record of praise for this young writer continues when he joins with Pádriac Reaney to co-edit a beautifully produced anthology of new Irish writing. The poets range from Máire Mhac an tSaoi to the new (to me) Tarlach MacCongáil. With prose from the erudite Alan Titley to the scholarly Seán Ó Tuama, the theme is focused in the opening poem by Nuala Ní Dhomhnaill: 'Ceist na Teangan'/ *The Language Question*. A language (there is no English text) illuminated by graphics, artwork and photos, striking images, including works by Reaney himself and two powerful sculptures by Cliodhna Cussen.

Claire Dagger's novel tells tales out of myths: archeologists beneath mysteries – time travel compulsory, enjoyable and undemanding. A minor disappointment when compiling the Irish Issue of *Chapman* (No 92) was the standard of Gaelic submissions. I admitted I was hasty when reviewing a bunch of titles from this Galway-based imprint in *Chapman* 93. More humble pie. A weekend at the 'Poetry Now Festival' in Dun Laoighaire in March 2000 was a revelation. Work from Ní Dhomhnaill, Louis De Paor and Rita Kelly had soul-searching depth. The organisers printed a complementary anthology (not priced). It includes new work from among many Patrick Galvin, Paul Durcan, Eva Bourke and Theo Dorgan. Write for a copy to Poetry Now 2000, Dun Laoighaire County Hall, Dun Laoighaire, Co Dublin, Ireland.

Hayden Murphy

Theatre Roundup

Scottish Playwrights featured prominently in both the autumn 1999 and spring 2000 seasons put on by many of the theatres in Scotland. They gave us spit-new plays, revamped older ones, adaptations and translations.

In September TAG toured Christopher Marlowe's *Doctor Faustus* in a new version by Edwin Morgan, a poet aware of the pains and paradoxes of this world. Morgan's text is like Marlowe's in verse, but Morgan adds contemporary as well as classical imagery and introduces two scenes set in Constantinople. The first is a wonderfully comic scene in the Sultan's harem and in the second the Genie, the Sultan and his Vizier show Faustus the Seven Deadly Things. Lucifer had earlier shown Faustus the Seven Deadly Sins, but these Seven Deadly Things are all products of modern science, Thalidomide, Anthrax, Lobotomy, Defoliation, Napalm, Meltdown, and Neutronbomb. They introduce themselves as if they are wonderful innovations which create beauty, their voices sounding like the doctor-scientists on TV programmes on GM food, infertility treatments or gene therapies – on message, but off morals.

The strength and chill of Marlowe's play comes from the awesomeness of Faustus selling his soul, his essential being, for temporal rather than eternal knowledge. It was written in a time where the belief in the terrors of hell and purgatory was much stronger. The challenge for a contemporary version of Faustus is to shake the audience into realising we may already be a modern day Faustus who has forgotten we made a pact we signed in our own blood. Morgan achieves this by linking *Doctor Faustus* clearly to modern times and our worldly desires, making a case for caution over earthy knowledge and its corruption. Unfortunately the production with the cast in camp costumes and platform shoes and too many scenes done in a pantomime style, made the play teeter on the verge of parody. I hope for another production which would leave the audience chastened and thoughtful; both Marlowe's and Morgan's texts deserve it.

David Greig's *The Cosmonaut's Last Message to the Woman He Once Loved in the Former Soviet Union* had its first Scottish production at the The Tron Glasgow, directed by Irina Brown before her resignation. It was a fine production of a complicated piece which interwove several separate stories across a two act play. Two cosmonauts circle the earth in their decaying space station called Harmony, whilst below a couple in a disintegrating marriage watch a TV which emits only white noise and, occasionally, the intermittent call signal from the space station. Only the husband hears the cosmonaut's calls, and builds a radio to reply. Again and again we listen to him broadcast "Is this Harmony?" But Harmony never hears him.

In all the characters there is a sense of the lack of real communication. There is a speech therapist trying to help a patient, whose words are falling away from her mind, until everything becomes stuff but not quite nonsense. As the patient lies on the "green stuff", patting it with pleasure, we feel and smell the grass she cannot say and we cannot see.

In the darker second half, one character has disappeared into the sea and his wife goes to France and finds a warm relationship with a man who understands her but not her words. One cosmonaut has spun off into his own orbit while the other is not rescued. His daughter, now kept by a businessman, remembers her father and looks for him in the sky. Usually I get irritated if relationships in an episodic play are not clear, but in *The Last Cosmonaut*, instead of irritating me, it underlined the theme of the fragility of language and loss.

Magnetic North, a new theatre company, brought Tom McGrath's latest play *The Dream Train,* directed by Nicholas Bone, to the Traverse. Subtitled "a play in counterpoint", it too explores harmony and interweaving of themes. It is set in the world of dreams and insomnia where extraordinary things occur as if they are totally normal. We encounter the insomniac Count who commissioned Bach to write *The Goldberg Varia-*

98

tions, and Bach's pupil who plays it to soothe the wakeful Count. As well as these two historical characters we meet several modern day people who drift between a a dream world and a wakeful one. With dialogue full of wit and uncertainty, this is a play which understands that audiences are intelligent, have a sense of humour and like having to think. Both McGrath's and Greig's plays show the strength of writing which has several themes, subtexts and sparse but significant information, where the signals are not obscured by the white noise.

'The Scottish Play' was done as the last Shakespeare at the Royal Lyceum of the millennium. Directed by Kenny Ireland, the set and lighting were monumental in effect, striking to see but they needed performances of operatic size. Unfortunately the actors, when not pushing the enormous blocks of scenery about, seem to have been asked to deliver their lines not as if they were communicating to one another but rather talking aloud to themselves. The result was that, except occasionally, their fates left us unmoved. There was little sense of the fatal steps by which Lady Macbeth and Macbeth himself, lead each other to destruction. In opera no singer is expected to move the scenery and sing but in theatre actors are often used as stage hands and then expected to deliver demanding texts. Scenery is never as important as actors, without actors the play cannot live. Directors and designers should remember that.

December found me hoping to see a *Peter Pan* to vanquish a previous adult encounter with *Peter Pan the Musical* starring Bonnie Langford. Stuart Paterson, writer of many fine children's plays, readapted the original story by Barrie rather than his subsequent play. Sadly the Royal Lyceum gave us a cheap-looking production where the Darling children were reduced to John and Wendy, the flying reduced to the minimum and the Lost Boys and John doubled as the Pirates. This last pairing (pun intended) caused much confusion in the audience as did the presentation of Tinkerbell as a constant bright red

laser light, not her shade I think, or as magical as a follow spot which can dim and brighten.

As the audience came out I heard too many parents saying "Wasn't that wonderful?" And the children were too polite to say no but they weren't smiling or trying to fly. Barrie's original play can and has switched on many small persons to the glorious magic world of make-believe that is theatre. Children don't have enough plays to go to. The few that we give them should be well produced and coherent in their casting and storytelling. We owe it to them and theatre's futures.

Stuart Paterson's play for adults *Mr Government* was done at the Royal Lyceum back in 1986. In December 1999 the Traverse Theatre Company produced his revised version retitled *King of the Fields,* directed by John Tiffany. Set in rural Ayrshire in the 30s, a prodigal son returns finds his younger brother tending the farm. At first it seems the older brother will bring a modernising dynamic to them both. But his brother's wife and his former sweetheart each bring pressures which he is not strong enough to handle. An extremely strong cast, production, direction and script gave us an intense night in the theatre where we saw every character confronted by their own flaws and desires. As each strove to resolve their separate dilemmas we saw their characters develop, for better or worse. This is a very fine play indeed.

Spring 2000 and the Traverse Theatre Company brought us Catherine Czerkawska's, *Quartz,* directed by Roxana Silbert. The set promised much as we walked through the sand and seaweed, smelling the sea scents which our feet released. In our seats we faced a set dominated by a huge Mobius Strip whose fold severely limited the acting area for the cast, as it was in Traverse Two. Sometimes the sets are too large for this space. When it is a travelling production there is some excuse, this was not. In Traverse One it could have looked superb.

The central character Michael is a hermit-like young man who lives contentedly by the seashore, gathering and polishing stones. His mother, Teresa has never given up hope that he would return to the church and become a priest. Michael's friend Claire harbours other hopes for him, that he will settle down with her. Pulled between these two women's desires, Michael finds an object washed up by the sea, made of stone, woman-sized and roughly human shaped. His mother sees it as a miracle, a carving of the Virgin Mary, there to confirm that Michael will become a priest. His reaction to the object's arrival is to see it as confirmation of the life he already leads. Teresa enlists her priest Father Sweeney, who, uncertain of his own faith is unable to curb the rampant excess of her beliefs. She turns Michael's place into a tawdry shrine. Claire tries again to pull him towards her but finally he destroys himself and the pathetic shrine.

The ideas of this play were potent but they weren't developed far enough. In choosing an uncommunicative central character Czerkawska has made it difficult for the audience to care about his anguish. Additionally Claire's emotions seemed more like a misplaced crush than a deep passion. We should have been able to see him positively through her desire. Faith and signs are mysterious, they empower people to do extraordinary things. Sadly this play felt underpowered for its themes and rather too ordinary. But then here on earth, *"we see through a glass darkly."*

Finally I went to see another version of a classic play by a Scottish playwright and poet, Liz Lochhead's version of Chekhov's *Three Sisters* at the Royal Lyceum, directed by Tony Cownie. Lochhead resets the play just after the war in Scotland; the longed-for Moscow becomes Oxford and the lover of the middle sister becomes a US officer. She makes the sisters and brother English, brought up in Scotland by their widowed father in the boarding school he owned and ran until he died. The play begins in their drawing room and conservatory, and as the sisters' grip on the house and school weakens the scenes shift to a former servant's bedroom and then to the grass outside.

The painful, strange atmosphere just after

WWII matched the *ennui* Chekhov created for his characters and in this production the sad only brother and his vile wife were well brought out. Here we watch tragedies develop as the brother gambles in his weakness and the sisters avoid love and betray others. At the end I found a lump in my throat at their collective painful futures. Only Nanny and the eldest sister seem to have found a possible harmony, though the middle sister and her steady husband who has always loved her seem to have the potential to find each other anew. The central question in the play "What is the point?" is one we go on asking ourselves as we too go through our disordered and varied lives.

In past months it has been possible at times to find the spirit of theatre alive and beating here in Scotland. In both new and old plays that spirit has been helping us to see ourselves and the world anew, confirming and challenging our hopes and fears. A good start as the centuries change over and we start again striving for harmony, despite our lack of understanding, of faith and of coherent meaning.

Thelma Good

Pamphleteer

Chapman receives dozens of new and long-established literary magazines every month. Whatever style of writing you fancy there is probably a publication waiting out there for you. But, while there are hundreds of magazines, not all of them are high quality, long-lived, easy to find or even printed regularly. This is because most are published by a solitary editor, churned out on a DTP machine and simply bound. The funding depends on subscriptions, the depths of the editor's own pocket or grants from various arts councils or other bodies. All these magazines deserve to be supported due to the hard work it takes to produce them, but it's difficult to decide which magazines to buy or subscribe to.

La Carta de Oliver (Luis M Campos 157 1609) Boulogne, Provincia de Buenos Aires, Argentina) is the most recent to fall onto my desk. A slim, bilingual volume (31 pages) produced in Argentina, I was struck by its quality. The paper is entirely touchable and the photographs sharp and evocative. However, the print size was too small and longer poems are crammed onto one page. Not all the texts are translated so you need Spanish to get through. Number 9, their spring edition, includes some Scottish poets: Norman Mac-Caig, Edwin Morgan, Iain Crichton Smith and Tessa Ransford. It's always refreshing to see cross-cultural work in any magazine and *La Carta de Oliver* gives insight into French, Swiss, Argentinian and American writing as well as a new view into more familiar names.

Another magazine that has caught my eye is *Heat* from Australia (PO Box 752, Artarmon, NSW 1570, Australia, £9 a single issue). I have read several issues and am amazed at the diversity and quality of the work. It has an international view with Southern Hemisphere bias, recent issues contain various Australia writers in Teheran, Franco-Spain and Moscow and a good mix of poetry, fiction and critical work from Indonesian, Trinidadian and Scottish (Robert Alan Jamieson's Shetland-dialect poetry) writers. It's a hefty, good read, but I was saddened to read in issue 14 that *Heat* would no longer be published after issue 16. It is disappointing to see that even large, well turned-out magazines have trouble keeping in the black. Subscribe or order a single copy of *Heat*, even if it is to catch the last light from a dying ember.

Frank (32, rue Edouard Valliant, 931000 Montreuil, France, £8.99 per issue) is another book-length, high-quality magazine. Their double issue 16/17 contains exciting titbits such as original letters from Henry Miller, and D H Lawrence, a look at writers from New Mexico, atmospheric black and white photographs and a wide selection of superb writing by Alexander Trocchi, John Calder and William Klein. If you can handle the price, this is a magazine to treasure.

Closer to home and one of several magazines connected with a university or college, new from St Andrews University, is *The Red Wheelbarrow* (School of English, Castle House, The Scores, St Andrews, Fife; £2 per issue). Issue Two contains work by familiar names such as John Burnside, Gael Turnbull and Don Paterson, but also rising stars such as Sally Evans, Anna Crowe and Ken Cockburn. This is not a Scottish only magazine, containing work by American, Venezuelan, Welsh and New Zealand writers, but its profile has a strong connection with the University. The magazine is simple in design but full of zest.

Nerve (Cardonald College, 690 Mosspark Drive, Glasgow G52 3AY, £9) is a good looking publication started last year. Issue 1 is a mix of poetry, fiction, reviews and drama, including names such as Des Dillon, Lesley Benzie and Jim Ferguson. There are some excellent illustrations alongside some of the work, but they are too small to get a real feel for them. I can see this publication developing into a strong showcase for Scottish writers.

Issue 2 and 3 of *GroundSwell* (22a Buccleuch Place, Edinburgh, £2.99) features 'names' like Edwin Morgan, Hanif Kureishi, Dilys Rose and Robert Alan Jamieson, but also contains work by the Craigmillar Literarcy Trust, Portobello High School and the Visible Ink writers' group, underlining their commitment to writing in the community. The editorial team is made up of Edinburgh University students who've put much work into this original and enjoyable publication.

The Coffee House (c/o Charnwood Arts, Fearon Hall, Rectory Road, Loughborough; 4.50 per year) calls itself The Meeting Place for the Arts and it does have a diverse, almost writing group, feel to it. These poems are not amateurish, there is some strong work by Lucien Stryk and Gillian Spraggs, but they are not all of the same quality. This sort of magazine brings writers of all levels together to share their work. They are great for beginning writers, to see a wide selection of poetry and also publish their own work for the first time. There are many magazines like this, connected with writers groups, local councils and schools. They come and go as funding is hard to maintain, but are essential as they provide a meeting place (in print) for a melting pot of writers which may simmer up talent.

The summer edition of *Red Lamp: The Journal of Realist, Socialist and Humanitarian Poetry* (5 Kahana Court, Mountain Creek, 4557 Queensland, Australia) includes poems on child labour, Hiroshima and imperialism. While the term 'cause' springs to mind, the editor Brad Evans manages to keep the magazine from becoming preachy. He says Red Lamp "is a literary vehicle by which ordinary people can voice their most honest and weighty opinions about society" and this is it's strength. The magazine is independent, not reliant on outside funding and includes no advertising, so the format is basic.

The Eildon Tree (Library Headquarters, St Mary's Mill, Selkirk TD7 5EW, £6) calls itself "a new writing magazine for the Scottish Borders" and is run by the local Writer-in-Residence Tom Bryan. It is aimed at and contains work by writers of the Scottish Borders. It contains a good selection of poetry and fiction, but also an article about self-published books by local writers and a feature on David Purves as their 'Scottish Borders Poet Profile'. As the magazine is still in its first year this policy of featuring local writers may change to widen the focus and increase subscription base. As it stands now it is a good outlet for beginning writers in the local area.

Another magazine with a regional connection is *The Broken Fiddle* (Macduff Arts Centre, Clergy Street, Macduff; no subscription prices given, £1.50 per issue). Sprinkled with Suzanne Gyseman's excellent illustrations, issue 11 features poetry, fiction and drama by Ian Stephen, Sheena Blackhall, Brian Johnston among others, many connected with the Aberdeenshire Writer-in-Residence. It is heavy on fiction (21 pages compared to 5 for poetry), giving poetry short shrift, dropped in at the back with several poems on one page. All the work, however, was entertaining.

Orbis is an excellent quarterly for writers. It has an informative Poetry Index giving up-to-date information on competitions, periodicals and poetry news. It also contains reviews,

letters to the magazine and a good selection of poetry. The featured poet is always eye-opening. *Orbis* recently celebrated its 30th anniversary and editor Mike Shields has to be congratulated for all his hard work.

A good way of finding out the latest small magazines is to check out The Small Press Guide (Writer's Bookshop). It contains over 300 entries on every kind of little magazine, fanzine and small poetry press you can imagine. It provides information on subscriptions, waiting times on submissions and payment details. This book is handy whether you want to submit your work or to subscribe.

AA Small Press Listings includes up to 700 magazines, updated regularly. Along with contact names, phone numbers, email and postal addresses, editors provide an editorial giving further information on their publications. HTML links to website and email addresses are included. The Listings are available as a Word 96 or 97 PC disc for £3 or as a email attachment £2. Contact Dee Rimbaud, AA Small Press Listings, 35 Falkland Street (GFL), Glasgow for more details.

The Association of Literary Magazines in Scotland (ALMS) was formed last year to promote public awareness of literary magazines and their contribution to our culture. ALMS's brings together the magazines, writers, bookshops, libraries and other literature organisations to promote Scottish literature across a wide a spectrum as possible. The 17 member magazines cover a wide range of Scottish literature and culture, focusing on regional writers (*NorthWords, Markings* and *Fife Lines*); promoting Scotland's native languages (*Gairm* and *Lallans*); the more established (like *Edinburgh Review, Cencrastus, Chapman*) and new names (*nomad, Deliberately Thirsty* and *Cutting Teeth*). ALMS's first project was to produce a high quality brochure featuring the magazines and give potential readers information about the magazines, subscription details and how to submit unsolicited work. The brochure and further details is available from ALMS, c/o *Chapman*, 4 Broughton Place, Edinburgh EH1 3RX.

Gerry Stewart

Catalogue

Many of the books here concern our favourite subject here at *Chapman* – writing. If there are books which can make you live till age 108 and become rich without leaving your living room, then why shouldn't there be books to teach you to write like Shakespeare? By far, the most worthwhile of these 'self-help' writing books is Pat Boran's, *The Portable Creative Writing Workshop* (Salmon Publishing £7.99), a practical guide which could benefit both beginners and experienced writers alike. The author, an award winning writer and editor, is honest about his goals, and doesn't make false promises of wealth and fame. The book takes the form of a series of games which are intended to stimulate the reader's creativity. It includes sections on poetry, fiction, as well as a chapter of advice from established writers such as Maeve Binchy and Eavan Boland giving directed advice to the beginner just starting out.

Not all 'self-help' writing books are up to this high standard. While every writer can use constructive criticism, I am suspicious of books which make dubious promises of commercial success. I instinctively feel there is something exploitative in books that are marketed like Louise Jordan's *How to Write For Children and Get Published* (Piatkus £9.99). While it is a well-written and directed book, the emphasis on publication implies a too-mechanical approach to the creative process.

I was also disappointed by David James' *Teach Yourself Letter Writing Skills* (Hodder & Stoughton £6.99). The irony of this book is that the 'model' letters used are actually quite poor examples of letter writing skills, many of them overly formal for today's use. Likewise, I was unimpressed by a chapter on e-mail writing skills. Discussing the rudimentary features of e-mails (ie delete, send, reply ...), the chapter is of minimal use to anyone with basic knowledge of the Internet. James writes, "before you can write to anyone, you must know their address. Now while addresses follow simple rules and are fairly easy to remember, you cannot work them out for yourself."

I am not quite sure which audience David Carter had in mind when he wrote *Teach Yourself How to Write a Play*. (Hodder & Stoughton £6.99). On one hand Carter assumes that we have all read Hamlet, Oedipus Rex and seen Amadeus, but on the other hand he explains the concepts of theme and plot at length. The book is clearly written, but the end result may be patronising for anyone with prior knowledge of the theatre.

How to Write About Yourself (Alison Chisholm & Brenda Courtie, £8.99) has some good, practical advice about gathering personal memoirs, and touches on elements of style, organization and format. It is fairly basic, as demonstrated by a chapter on 'clarity rules', which includes detailed lessons on grammar and punctuation; this should be unnecessary for the more experienced writer.

If you want a step by step guide to the publishing process, then have a look at Janet MacDonald's *Teach Yourself Writing Non-Fiction* (Hodder & Stoughton £6.99); a well written introductory guide to marketing non-fiction work. The author's own experience in the non-fiction market is in writing about horses and side saddles. There are numerous references to this throughout, becoming excessive for those of us without horse-sense.

A quick subject-detour will bring us to *Drugs and the Party Line* (Kevin Williamson, Canongate £5.99); a well-argued and intelligently written book on the drug war in Scotland. In a pocket-sized format, Williamson discusses the different approaches to dealing with the pervasiveness of class A drugs in this country. The author admits he is involved in the 'harm reduction' campaign, and this book is unmistakably a political treatise, devoted to criticising the government's attempts at prohibition. Nevertheless, the arguments he puts forth are strong, and backed up with solid statistics, making even a SAD (Scotland Against Drugs) campaigner think twice.

Perverts, fetishes, and homo-erotic art;

these are just some of the issues touched on in *The Passionate Camera* (ed. Deborah Bright, Routledge £18.99); a racy compilation of writings and photographs. This collection is intended to document the history of same-sex love. David Deitcher writes,

All too often, the historic traces of same-sex love consist in entries in police records and court documents, or stigmatizing evaluations by physicians, psychologists and criminologists. Thus the history of gay desire has been written by individuals and institutions whose purpose has been to snuff it out.

This is a impressive volume of work, but some of the writing is quite dense. The topics vary, ranging from specific artists' work such as David Wojnarowicz's 'Arthur Rimbaud in New York' to accounts of political activism such as Erica Rand's campaign directed to dykes (yes, this is the politically correct term) to increase the visibility of lesbians.

On the subject of dikes, Scottish Cultural Press has released *The Dream of Night Fishers* (John Rice, £7.99), a beautiful collection of poems and black and white photographs depicting elements of Scottish landscape such as the sea, rocks, cattle and, yes, dikes. In keeping with the theme, *Nis Aosmhor* (Acair, Photographs Dan Morrison) is a handsome book of quality black and white photographs portraying the landscape, tradition, and customs in the rural community of postwar Ness. In the forward, Donald Macleod poignantly writes,

these photographs are sharply focused on one time and one place . . . they sum up the Hebridean attitude to the outside world: amusement, compliance and confrontation.

Formal and candid photos are included in this collection; all stamped with the mark of an isolated, but healthy and active community.

And for those of you who can't get enough of the Hebrides, Acair has re-released two more books on the subject. A new edition of *The Book of Barra* is available with a fresh cover; it is a compilation of writings about the island by locals, travellers, and historians. *Lewis; The Story of an Island* is also available in a pocket-sized format. Written by a native of the island, Christine Macdonald, this book covers the history, literature and music among other topics relating to life on Lewis.

Revolutionary Empire (Angus Calder, Pimlico £15) is not just another book on Britain's imperial history; it attempts to connect historical events outside Britain with happenings within the Isles. The story begins in the 1400s period of expansion and spans the revolutions of the 1700s. Each period is treated with an in-depth account of overseas and domestic activities, as well as the intellectual history of the time. This is a large book, densely packed with information, but Calder's skilled writing makes it a pleasant read.

A State of Independence (£9.95 ed. Tony Frazer) is a wonderful compilation of work by 18 very different poets, all of whom have been published in a wide range of British journals and presses. This is not a compilation of mainstream British poetry, as it includes lesser known poets such Catherine Walsh, Lee Harwood and Grace Lake.

To Shirk No Idleness; A Critical Biography of the Poet Andrew Young (Edward Lowbury and Alison Young, Salzburg University Press) doesn't have the looks, but certainly has the personality. The cover and design are fairly spartan, but the text more than makes up for this, in a revealing analysis of the poet's life. The authors, Young's daughter and son-in-law, spare no element of his life, giving the reader a sincere and detailed account of Andrew Young's poetic life.

Edinburgh University Press has released the first modern edition of Walter Scott's *Guy Mannering* (£30.00). Unique to this handsome volume is Scott's graphic depiction of characters from the Edinburgh literary scene. New from Clydeside Press is *Untold Stories; Remembering Clydebank in War Time* (£4.50); a compilation of individual narratives and telling photographs from the Clydebank blitz. And lastly, Weidenfeld & Nicolson have released *Arthur and the Lost Kingdoms* by Alistair Moffat (£20.00), a carefully researched book about the legendary Arthur of Celtic mythology.

Notes on Contributors

Dag T Andersson (born 1945), teaches philosophy at the University of Tromsö, Norway. Has published books and articles on Walter Benjamin and on philosophy and literature. Is currently writing a book on John Ruskin's Philosophy of Seeing.

Iain Bahlaj, 21, lives in Lochgelly, Fife. He writes frantically in a bid to escape. He hopes to eventually blank out life with booze and drugs. His first book may be released by Pulp Books.

George Bruce was born in 1909 in Fraserburgh. His first collection of poems, *Sea Talk* (1944) written during WWII, drew its imagery of survival from the community of the seatown. His most recent collection *Pursuit: Poems 1986-98*, (1999) was published for his 90th birthday. It won the Saltire Book of the Year award 2000.

Paul Brownsey is a philosophy lecturer at Glasgow University whose stories have appeared in various magazines and anthologies.

John Burnside has published six books of poetry, of which the most recent are *A Norman Skin* and *Swimming in the Flood*, and two novels, *The Dumb House* and *The Mercy Boys*. His new collection of poems, *The Asylum Dance* will be published by Jonathan Cape in 2000, alongside a collection of stories, entitled *Burning Elvis*.

Angus Calder recently published Wars, an anthology of poetry and verse about warfare in the 20th century with Penguin.

Aimée Chalmers has had little opportunity to use the Scots language in her working life, so she's making up for it now.

Linda Cracknell's first story to be published 'Life Drawing' won the Macallan/ Scotland on Sunday Short Story Competition in 1998. Her first collection will be published in 2001.

Katrina Crosbie is an Adult Education writing tutor at Leith Academy, and has had stories published in magazines and anthologies such as *New Writing Scotland*, *The New Writer* and *West Coast Magazine*. She was shortlisted for the 1997 Ian St James Awards.

Colin Dunbar has recently had a residency exhibition at the Edinburgh Printmakers Workshop. His portrait of George Bruce received a commendation from the Morrison Portrait Award Exhibition at the RSA.

George Gunn was born and lives in Thurso, Caithness where he is currently artistic director of the Grey Coast Theatre Company. He broadcasts regularly on *BBC Radio 4* and *Radio Scotland*. His latest book of poetry is called *In the Pictish Navy*.

Robin Hamilton Educated in Glasgow, and recently retired from Loughborough Univeristy. Collected poems, *The Lost Jockey*, published in 1985. The poems in this issue are from a recently completed sequence, *Stamping on Schrodinger's Kittens*.

Roddy Hamilton lives in Aberdeen. He has had work published in *New Writing Scotland* and various publications. He is currently completing his second novel, entitled *Omm*.

Tom Hubbard is currently visiting assistant professor of literature and language at the University of North Carolina at Asheville. His most recent book is *The Integrative Vision: Poetry and the Visual Arts in Baudelaire, Rilke and MacDiarmid* (Akros 1997).

John Law is T S Law's elder son, an works at sortin computers. He wis a co-foonder of the Scots Language Resource Centre in Perth, and in Editor o Lallans magazine evenou.

Thomas Sturdy Law wis brocht up in a minin faimlie in Newarthill, an wrocht as airframe fitter, miner and technical writer. He mairiet Peggy MacPhail an haed twa sons John and Andrew. The lairge body o his 50 years' makkin bydes maistlie unpublished as yet, though a major collection will kythe later this year.

Irfan Merchant lives and works in Edinburgh. Sometimes he wonders about himself.

David McVey is from Kirkintilloch and works at Paisley University. He has had many short stories published, including one in the Flamingo *New Scottish Writing 1998*.

Hayden Murphy born 1945 Dublin. Poet and arts journalist based in Edinburgh. Guest Editor Irish Issue *Chapman* (Nos 19 and 92).

William Oliphant is a retired electronics engineer, once known for repairing electronic keyboards in the Glasgow area. He started writing poetry in 1983 shortly before his 63rd birthday, having previously some reputation as a short story writer.

Janet Paisley most recent collection *Ye Cannae Win* has been published by *Chapman* as a part of their new *Wild Women Series*.